A KALEIDOSCOPE KIDS® BOOK

Skyscrapers!

SUPER STRUCTURES TO DESIGN & BUILD

Carol A. Johmann

Illustrations by
Michael Kline

WILLIAMSON PUBLISHING • CHARLOTTE, VT

Library of Congress Cataloging-in-Publication Data

Johmann, Carol A., 1949-
    Skyscrapers! : super structures to design & build / Carol A. Johmann ; illustrations by Michael Kline.
      p. cm. — (A Williamson Kaleidoscope Kids book)
    Includes index.
    ISBN 1-885593-50-3 (pbk.)
      1. Skyscrapers—Juvenile literature. [1. Skyscrapers.] I. Kline, Micheal P., ill. II. Title.

TH1615 .J65 2001
720'.483—dc21
                                                      2001025838

Kaleidoscope Kids® Series Editor: **Susan Williamson**
Project Editor: **Vicky Congdon**
Illustrations: **Michael Kline**
Design: **Black Fish Design: Christy Amlicke, Joseph Lee,
        Aaron Schneider**
Printing: **Quebecor World**

Printed in Canada

Williamson Publishing Co.
P.O. Box 185
Charlotte, Vermont 05445
1-800-234-8791

10 9 8 7 6 5 4 3 2 1

Little Hands®, *Kids Can!*®, *Tales Alive!*®, and *Kaleidoscope Kids*®
are registered trademarks of Williamson Publishing.

Good Times™ and *Quick Starts for Kids!*™ are trademarks of
Williamson Publishing.

DEDICATION

To my grandmother, Florence Heath, and great-uncle, Al Waterman, who took me to the top of a skyscraper for the first time, and to my nephew, Matthew Croteau, who is the same age now as I was then. He loves construction sites and building things, and will have a ball watching his own skyscraper go up!

ACKNOWLEDGMENTS

Many thanks to Deborah Besser, P.E., Assistant Professor of Engineering at the University of Wisconsin-Stout, for reading the manuscript and offering valuable suggestions. Any mistakes still remaining are mine, not hers. Thanks also to Vicky Congdon for her superb editorial work and to Susan Williamson for more of the same; to my sister, Elizabeth Rieth, who didn't co-author this time but was there for support and as a sounding board; and to my niece and nephew, Christine and David Rieth, as usual, for their help with the activities.

Photography: cover, Chrysler Building, Digital Imagery © copyright 2001 Photodisc, Inc.; page 4, New York City skyline, Digital Imagery © copyright 2001 Photodisc, Inc; page 6, Home Insurance Building, Chicago Historical Society, ICHi-20637; page 7, Auditorium Building, Jeffery Howe; page 8, Reliance Building, Library of Congress, HABS, ILL, 16-CHIG, 30-1; page 8, Flatiron Building, Black Fish Design; page 11, Norwest Center, Steve Bergerson; page 14, Empire State Building, Carl Forster; page 16, Sears Tower, GreatBuildings.com © Artifice Images; page 17, John Hancock Tower, Susan Murie, courtesy of iboston.org; page 19, Equitable Building, Collection of the New-York Historical Society, negative number 49539; page 21, Fleet Bank Plaza, Black Fish Design; page 31, AutoCAD illustration, Scott Libert; page 32, Citicorp Center, Black Fish Design; page 33, supercolumn of Citicorp Center, Black Fish Design; page 35, Lipstick Building, Black Fish Design; page 35, Marina City, Mary Ann Sullivan, Bluffton College; page 36, Petronas Towers, GreatBuildings.com © Anton Bocaling; page 38, Woolworth Building, Jeffery Howe; page 38, Woolworth Building detail, Mary Ann Sullivan, Bluffton College; page 39, Chrysler Building, Black Fish Design; page 49, Rialto Towers, Melbourne Observation Deck, Melbourne, Australia; page 49, Transamerica Building, Digital Imagery © copyright 2001 Photodisc, Inc; page 51, steel-yard, Black Fish Design; page 57, tower crane, American Tower Crane, Inc.; page 57, three workers securing a rivet, Photography Collection, Miriam and Ira D. Wallach Division of Art, Prints & Photographs, The New York Public Library, Astor, Lenox and Tilden Foundations; page 70, Elisha Otis demonstrating the safety brake, Otis Elevator Company; page 73, Scotia Plaza, kenzingtonphotos.com © Colin Kent; page 83, Empire State Building lobby, kenzingtonphotos.com © Michael Warford; page 84, Rockefeller Plaza, Digital Imagery © copyright 2001 Photodisc, Inc; page 88, The Mile-High Illinois, The drawings of Frank Lloyd Wright are Copyright © 1957, 1994, 2001 The Frank Lloyd Wright Foundation, Scottsdale, AZ.

Contents

Reach for the Sky

Skyscraper — it's the perfect word for those super-tall buildings that soar out of the ground like shooting rockets! From afar, skyscrapers really do seem to "scrape the sky." And that view! On a clear day from the top of the Empire State Building in New York City, you can see into the four neighboring states — as well as the lower part of New York. The people on the street look like ants, and the clouds and fog drift by *below* you! The view from the ground up can be dizzying. Skyscrapers are *huge* and sometimes overwhelming. Like mountain cliffs facing each other across a river, they turn our city streets into canyons of steel, glass, and concrete.

Skyscrapers provide offices and apartments for millions of people all over the world. Many skyscrapers have shops, post offices, restaurants, pools, and health clubs. Some even have their own zip codes! They are complete communities that reach up instead of spreading out.

New York City skyline • New York, NY

Born in the USA

The story of the skyscraper begins in 1871 with a huge fire that destroyed much of Chicago. To make room for all the people and businesses that suddenly needed shelter, architects began designing buildings with more and more stories. Just 20 years after the fire, Chicago was full of a new style of construction known as the skyscraper. Then, New York City started building skyward, and now it probably has more famous skyscrapers than any other city in the world!

From Stone To Steel

Of course, it wasn't enough for people in Chicago to just say, "Hey, let's start putting up taller buildings." A new vision in building design had to come first, followed by innovations in techniques and materials to make the vision a reality.

Older tall structures, like cathedrals and towers, had been built of masonry (stone or bricks). Even the "big" buildings of the early 1800s — the five- and six-story office buildings, hotels, and warehouses — were stone structures. The walls held up the building, so they had to be thicker at the bottom to support the weight of the upper stories. Any openings made these buildings weaker, so windows were small. Imagine how gloomy and cramped it must have been inside, especially on the lower floors!

To build masonry walls that were stronger but at the same time thinner, architects began using iron beams. But iron is brittle and can break under the weight of a really tall building. Then, in the 1880s, came the idea — and the material — that made it possible to build taller, more graceful structures with roomier interiors and larger windows. The material was steel. The engineering concept was to build a frame of steel beams that was so strong the walls could just hang from it. The frame, not the walls, would hold up the building. And windows could be any size you wanted!

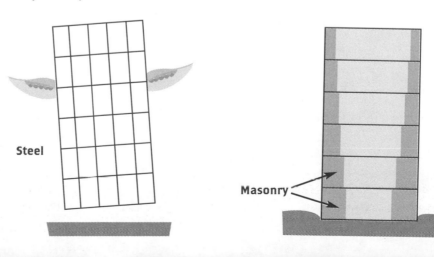

Steel

Masonry

TALL THINKERS

William Jenney and the Steel Frame

One day in the early 1880s, so the story goes, engineer **William Le Baron Jenney** was in his office trying to figure out a way to provide the lower floors of an office building with as much space and light as the upper floors. Frustrated and unable to solve the problem, Jenney went home. Just as he walked in, his wife closed the large book she'd been reading and placed it on top of a wire birdcage. Jenney stared at the cage. If a thin wire cage could hold up a heavy book, maybe a steel cage, or *frame*, could hold up a tall building!

Jenney went on to design and build the 10-story *Home Insurance Building* in 1885 in Chicago. Although there were other buildings in Chicago and New York that were just as tall, the Home was the first to use both steel and iron beams in its frame *and* it was the first building in which the walls and floors were completely supported by the frame.

Home Insurance Building • Chicago, IL • 1885

Mass-Produced Steel Is Here!

Steel, an exceptionally strong but lightweight metal, is made by blasting air through melted iron to remove impurities. It was the perfect framing material to take big buildings to new heights. But in the early 1800s, steel was very expensive to produce. So when British engineer **Henry Bessemer** and American iron manufacturer **William Kelly** each invented similar ways to produce large amounts of steel cheaply, they revolutionized the construction industry. By 1880, the U.S. was producing close to 1.2 million tons (1.1 t) of steel a year, using what became known as the *Bessemer process*.

The Sky's the Limit!

With the innovation of the steel frame, skyscrapers were structurally ready to take off. But a few other inventions were needed before building them was really practical.

Fire protection and wind bracing were necessary. Electricity certainly helped. Power equipment like excavators, bulldozers, and cranes were important, to dig deep holes for secure foundations and lift pieces of the frame into place. But one machine was more important than all the rest. It had nothing to do with building skyscrapers, but rather made living in them much easier. Can you guess what it was?

Auditorium Building • Chicago, IL • 1889

TALL THINKERS

Louis Sullivan and the First Style of Skyscrapers

In the early days of skyscraper construction, architects designed the outer walls to hide the structure underneath. From the outside, the buildings looked just like the older large buildings that were made of stone. **Louis Sullivan**, who worked under William Jenney early in his career, believed that the outside of a skyscraper should reveal its interior. In his designs (like the *Auditorium Building* in Chicago), the stone on the outside shows where the steel columns are. His ideas helped define the first style of skyscrapers known as the *Chicago School* (1880–1900).

Answer: The elevator. After all, you wouldn't want to climb hundreds of steps to get to the top floors, would you?

SUPER 'SCRAPERS!

The Earliest Skyscrapers

Jenney's Home Insurance Building was taken down in 1931, but you can still see some of the other early skyscrapers. You probably won't gasp in awe at this building today, but back in 1894, when the 15-story *Reliance Building* in Chicago was constructed, people were amazed not just by its height but by its windows! It was the first building to have an all-steel frame, so each floor could have huge windows that wrapped around the building, letting in lots of light and air.

Eight years later, the 20-story *Flatiron Building* was astonishing people in New York City. Not only is the building site triangular, the actual building is triangular as well! At first, New Yorkers worried that this unusual building might topple over. Today it's New York's oldest surviving skyscraper, a striking example of the decorative exterior popular in the early 1900s.

Reliance Building • Chicago, IL • 1894

Flatiron Building • New York, NY • 1902

1894
Construction of the 15-story Reliance Building in Chicago, the first building with an all-steel frame

1895
New York takes the lead with the American Surety Building, also 22 stories but three feet (1 m) taller than the Masonic Temple

1885
William Le Baron Jenney completes the 10-story Home Insurance Building in Chicago, the first to use steel beams for part of its frame

1892
Chicago shows off the 22-story Masonic Temple at the World's Columbian Exposition, the second U.S. world's fair. It was the last Chicago building to hold the title of tallest until the Sears Tower was completed in 1974!

Earliest to be called a skyscraper
Burnham and Root's Montauk Block

1881
Construction of the Montauk Block, Chicago's first 10-story building and one of the earliest to be called a skyscraper

1882
Thomas Edison turns electric lights on from a central power station in New York City

1871
The Great Chicago Fire

1870
The first passenger elevator is installed in the Equitable Assurance Society Building in New York City

1857
Elisha Otis builds the first elevator safe enough for passengers

1856
Henry Bessemer patents his process for producing steel

Shaping City Skylines

By the 1920s, the distinctive skyline created by New York City's giant towers was the first thing people saw when coming into the harbor by ship. Today most major cities around the world boast skyscrapers, and many besides New York City and Chicago can be recognized by their skylines. Skyscrapers add magic to a city, attracting people from far and wide.

Ready to Reach for the Sky?

Would you like to be a builder of skyscrapers — perhaps an architect, an engineer, or a construction worker?

Then imagine yourself in the middle of a big, busy city in front of a hole so huge it takes up a whole city block. Your job is to fill that hole — and the space above it — with a building that will truly scrape the sky. Along the way, you'll create a model city, design a skyscraper, and meet the people you need to build it. You'll build girders, a crane, and an elevator as you learn about the materials and equipment that make skyscrapers possible. You'll see how to put it all together so your skyscraper stands tall. And, once it's done, you'll discover what it's like to live and work inside a building that sways in the wind as it towers above the ground. So, come along, stretch your mind and imagination, and begin reaching for the sky!

Before Building Begins

Before a bulldozer digs a shovelful of earth and years before anyone moves in, before a crane lifts a single steel beam, all sorts of people start planning. They decide what the skyscraper will be used for — will people live in it, work in it, or will it have many uses? The *John Hancock Center* in Chicago, for example, has offices, apartments, and a hotel. How tall should the skyscraper be? Are 50 stories enough? 70? 100? What should it look like? And which design will best suit the building's uses and the neighborhood's architectural style?

These are the easier issues to deal with. The architects, owners, and engineers also consider the skyscraper's location and its impact on the neighborhood. Is the desired site empty or will an older building have to be torn down first? How will a new building fit in with its surroundings? Will it cause too much traffic, overload electricity and water supplies, or block the sun from the streets below? What materials should be used? Who will do all the work to build it and then to keep it running? And how much will everything cost? Whew! Forget about building a skyscraper, just *planning* one is a huge job!

"Before beginning the design for Norwest Center, we took long walks, exploring the city to get a feel for its special qualities. We saw that many Minneapolis buildings are warm beige, a good color for long winters. A building is a piece of a city, so its design must be based on how it will affect the city."
—CESAR PELLI, ARCHITECT

Norwest Center • Minneapolis, MN • 1988

The Planning Phase: Who Does What

Thousands of people work together in different teams on different jobs at different times to build a skyscraper. Here are the people involved in the planning phase.

The OWNER (rarely one person, most often a large company) decides what the skyscraper will be used for and pays for it to be built. The owner also selects and buys the land, or *site*, hires the architect, and approves the design.

The architect works with STRUCTURAL ENGINEERS to design the building's frame and foundation. ELECTRICAL ENGINEERS design the electrical systems, and MECHANICAL ENGINEERS design the HVAC (heating, ventilation, and air-conditioning systems) and the plumbing. These teams of specialists make thousands of *blueprints* — drawings that show the site, the design, and every part of the building.

The ARCHITECT designs the skyscraper, determining its height and shape, choosing its style, and selecting the building materials to fulfill her creative vision of the building.

SURVEYORS check that the property lines at the site are correct and note special features of the land, like slopes or wet spots.

The GEOTECHNICAL ENGINEERS, who know all about different soils and rock formations below the earth's surface, gather information that the structural engineers will use to design the foundation.

CITY PLANNERS review the plans to ensure that they meet city building and safety *codes*, or requirements. Before giving the owner permission to build, city planners confirm that the city can provide adequate services such as water, electricity, fire and police protection, and sewage and waste disposal.

Once plans are approved, the architect asks several construction companies for estimates of costs and time, called *bids*, to build the skyscraper. The BUILDER, also called the GENERAL CONTRACTOR, is responsible for all construction details, such as getting materials to the site on schedule, hiring workers, and scheduling jobs.

Make a Plan of Action

A nearby park needs to be cleaned up. Litter must be collected, the grass needs to be mowed, and the flower beds have to be weeded and replanted. Plan and organize an effort to get the park back in shape!

Start with a list of the jobs to be done, friends who will help, and the tools you'll need. To design your plan of action, consider things like: In what order will the jobs need to be done? How long will each job take? Do you need contributions of supplies, like flowers? Do you need any adult help or supervision? Then, divide your friends into teams, select a leader for each team, and assign a team to each job.

Now that you've got such a great plan, use it! Call the mayor's office or the local town offices and find out if there's a park or playground nearby that could use your help. Then, round up your friends!

SUPER 'SCRAPERS!

Teamwork and the Empire State Building

A lot of cooperation and organization made the most famous skyscraper of all, New York City's 102-story *Empire State Building*, possible. Architects, owners, and builders worked together so well that they got the job done ahead of schedule *and* under budget!

In less than 20 months, all these things (and more) were done:

- 6,000 workers were hired
- A famous hotel on the site was demolished
- The site was *excavated* (dug) and the foundation laid
- 60,000 tons (54,420 t) of steel were delivered to the site and used to build the frame
- 103 concrete floors were poured
- 10 million bricks were laid as backing for the limestone walls
- 73 elevators (67 passenger and 6 freight) and 7 miles (11.3 km) of elevator shaft were installed
- 6,500 windows were set
- 6,700 radiators and 2,500 toilets and sinks were installed
- Walls were plastered and painted
- The lobby was decorated in marble

And on May 1, 1931, everyone celebrated the completion of the Empire State Building with a grand party. President Hoover officially opened the building by pressing a button in Washington, D.C. to turn on the lights!

Empire State Building • New York, NY • 1931

No Plan? Uh-Oh!

Imagine the chaos there would be if general contractors didn't plan ahead and schedule every job. Workers who pour the concrete floors might show up before the workers who put up the steel frame. The wrong materials might be delivered or the walls might get plastered before the plumbing was finished. (Oops! No restrooms on that floor!)

Go back to your park clean-up project (page 13). The Parks and Recreation Department has agreed to donate a swing set. A local garden club has offered to build some wooden planters, and a Girl Scout troop has volunteered to plant flowers.

Now you'll really need that plan! Revise your original list, adding the new tasks in the order in which they need to happen — you don't want the Girl Scouts arriving before the planters are ready.

For some jobs (like setting the swing set in concrete), you'll need help, so be sure those teams have one or two adults on them.

Make a list of everything you'll need and when you'll need it. A drawing of your site is a good idea, too, so that the swing set doesn't get put in the perfect sunny spot for the flower bed. You'll be amazed at how smoothly things run when you organize them ahead of time (but expect mass confusion if you don't!).

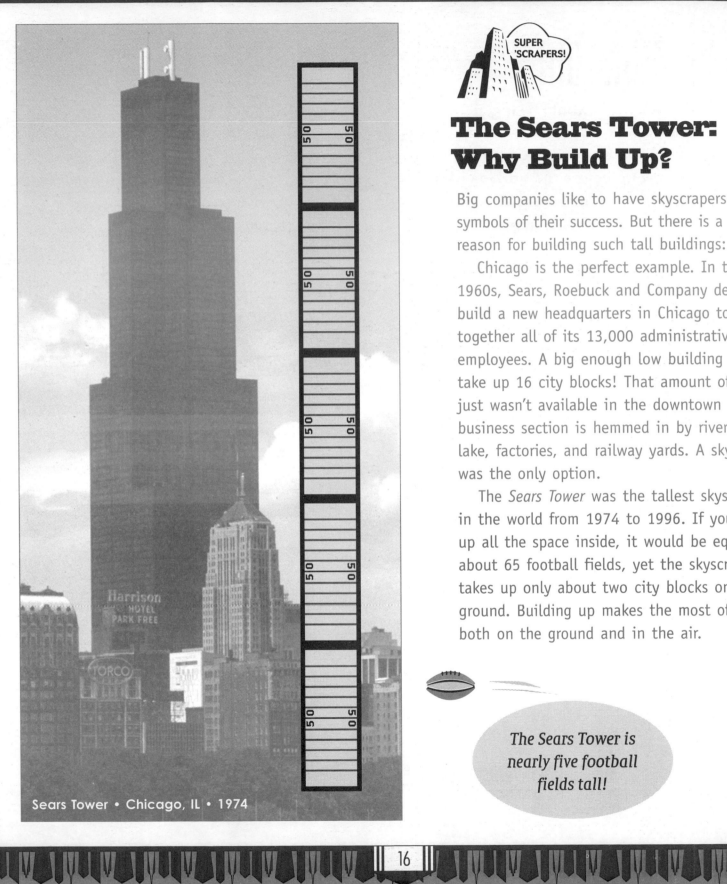

Sears Tower • Chicago, IL • 1974

SUPER 'SCRAPERS!

The Sears Tower: Why Build Up?

Big companies like to have skyscrapers as symbols of their success. But there is a practical reason for building such tall buildings: space.

Chicago is the perfect example. In the late 1960s, Sears, Roebuck and Company decided to build a new headquarters in Chicago to bring together all of its 13,000 administrative employees. A big enough low building would take up 16 city blocks! That amount of land just wasn't available in the downtown area. Its business section is hemmed in by rivers, a lake, factories, and railway yards. A skyscraper was the only option.

The *Sears Tower* was the tallest skyscraper in the world from 1974 to 1996. If you added up all the space inside, it would be equal to about 65 football fields, yet the skyscraper takes up only about two city blocks on the ground. Building up makes the most of space, both on the ground and in the air.

The Sears Tower is nearly five football fields tall!

SUPER 'SCRAPERS!

The John Hancock Tower: New Reflects Old

Covered in mirrored glass from bottom to top, the 60-story *John Hancock Tower* in Boston stands in stark contrast to the historic buildings like Trinity Church and Boston Public Library (both built in the late 1800s) at its feet. Yet, by reflecting them in its walls, it embraces them, too.

With his dramatic, elegant buildings that combine geometric shapes and lots of glass, the architect, **I. M. Pei,** refined the *glass-box* skyscraper style that became popular in the 1950s and 1960s. These stark, very modern-looking skyscrapers typically combine a glass exterior and lots of sleek metal with sheer size for impact.

Today the Hancock Tower is a symbol of beauty and grace. During the building's construction, however, it was famous for popping windows — it seemed as though the wind was blowing them right out of the building! Cracking the mystery of the Hancock windows took a long time. But years later, it turned out it wasn't the wind after all. The building's windows (two panes of glass stuck together with special lead tape to help insulate the building) were the largest of their kind ever used. Unfortunately, the weight of the huge

John Hancock Tower • Boston, MA • 1976

panes plus the sun's heat caused the tape to rip away from the glass, leaving tiny cracks. When the wind blew and the building swayed, the cracks got bigger and the windows broke, crashing down to the sidewalk below.

What Does a 'Scraper Do to the Sun?

Arrange the boxes like a street full of skyscrapers (stack some to make really tall 'scrapers) and place the "pedestrians" on the streets and sidewalks. Darken the room and shine the flashlight at the boxes, moving the light as if the sun were rising in the morning, high above at noon, and then setting in the late afternoon.

Compare the shadows created by the different boxes throughout your flashlight "day." What shapes cast the largest shadows? What arrangement of shapes creates the most daylight? If you were living next to a skyscraper, what shape and height would you most prefer?

***Note:** Leave your arrangement of boxes set up. You'll need them again.*

Materials

→ Boxes and cartons of different sizes and shapes (cereal, oatmeal, cracker)
→ Toy characters or action figures
→ Flashlight

Where's my Barbie?

"Bring Back the Sun!"

By 1892, Chicago had many buildings that rose 10 to 20 stories straight up from the edge of the street. People complained that they never saw the sun and that the streets were dark and gloomy. No light entered the windows of nearby lower buildings. So for many years, the city had laws restricting the height of new buildings to just 130 feet (40 m), or about 10 stories — way too low for tall skyscrapers.

New York City didn't have building restrictions until 1916. That was just one year after the giant 39-story *Equitable Building* went up. New Yorkers thought it was so ugly and big that it might be a menace to public health and safety. After all, its shadow was four blocks long! The citizens' outrage (and the even larger buildings in the works) led New York City to regulate skyscrapers. From then on, really tall buildings had to have a stepped appearance, like a staircase. The "steps," called *setbacks*, let more sunshine and air through.

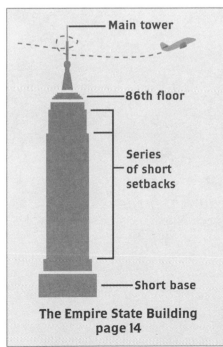

Main tower

86th floor

Series of short setbacks

Short base

The Empire State Building page 14

Setback Solutions

Setbacks make the top of a skyscraper seem farther away and the whole building look taller than it really is. Think of the way a mountain slopes upward to a peak. Most important, because the building is less bulky, more light gets down to the street below.

Equitable Building • New York, NY • 1915

Build a Setback Skyscraper

Go back to your street of buildings on page 18. Choose two buildings that are the same height. Shine a flashlight down on them and notice how much light reaches the street. Using smaller boxes (jewelry, Jell-O), redesign one building to have setbacks. Build the other building up to the same height without setbacks. Now, shine the flashlight down on the street. Compare the shadows of the two buildings. Where does more light reach the street?

What Zone Are You In?

Today, most towns and cities have regulations about the kinds of buildings that may be constructed in each neighborhood. These rules determine what kinds of businesses (for example, light manufacturing, heavy manufacturing, or office work) are permitted in the area, how tall a building may be, even what it may look like. Sometimes the rules allow for a mix of businesses and houses in certain areas. Such rules are called *zoning laws.*

Try it! *Call your town or city clerk to find out about the zoning laws in your neighborhood. For fun, ask if a fast-food restaurant could be built on the street where you live. Could you put up a permanent big bright purple sign in your front yard? Could you paint your house in red, white, and blue stripes or in black and red squares like a checkerboard? How would you feel if your house were all on one floor and a neighbor wanted to build a three-story house next door?*

Skyscrapers and Urban Spaces

Skyscrapers have not only changed the way cities look, but also how people live in urban areas. Cities now have large downtown business sections with buildings packed closely together, surrounded by areas where people live in tall apartment buildings. The tall buildings of New York City make it possible for millions of people to work and live in a small area, but it also makes the city very crowded.

In addition to considering the size and shape of the buildings, city planners and zoning administrators require architects to incorporate plazas and other open spaces, fountains, sculpture, benches, and plantings to help keep urban spaces more inviting and to calm people's frazzled nerves from honking horns, construction, sirens, and hordes of people rushing from place to place.

TAKE THE CHALLENGE!

Design and Build a Model City

Before architects design a skyscraper, they spend time in the city where it will be built so they have a sense of the city's personality (see quote, page 11). To get a feeling for the "city" where your skyscraper will be, why not construct a model section of it.

(see quote, page 11)

Materials

- ➔ Pencil and paper (graph paper helps)
- ➔ Large piece of sturdy cardboard or foam board for base
- ➔ Boxes, tubes, and containers of various sizes and shapes for buildings (your collection of boxes from the activity on page 18)
- ➔ Flashlight
- ➔ Masking tape
- ➔ Scissors
- ➔ Black, green, and blue construction paper
- ➔ Toothpicks

1 *Draw a street plan, including at least one main street and several side streets. (The city blocks don't have to be square.) Will traffic move efficiently through the neighborhood? Are there sidewalks? What about parking lots, bus stops, and taxi stands?*

2 *Now, sketch in places to eat, shop, play, and work. You'll need a mix of office and apartment buildings. Include at least two or three older historic buildings, as well as some modern "high-rises." Ask people who work in a city what they like about the area and* *what they wish it had.*

3 *Think about a site, or location, for the skyscraper you will build later in the book. The site (and your skyscraper) can be any shape. For example, one skyscraper in Chicago curves around a bend in the Chicago River, while one in*

New York City is a narrow rectangle squeezed in between an avenue and the Hudson River. Incorporate the site for your 'scraper into your model city.

4 Now, sketch your final plan on the cardboard base. Arrange the boxes, tubes, and containers along the streets to create the buildings. Vary their height, size, and distance from the sidewalk, according to how you envision them being used. If something isn't working, move it around.

5 Now, use a flashlight to check the shadows the buildings make. Does your plan allow enough sunlight to reach the streets and lower buildings? Redesign some of your buildings with setbacks, if necessary.

6 Imagine walking down each street. How would it feel? Closed in and dark? Or light and airy? Would you feel safe? Did you include any small parks or gardens to give people relief from all the concrete? Are there any playgrounds? Would you want to live in this neighborhood? Make any changes you think are necessary.

7 When you're satisfied that you have a people-friendly design, tape the buildings to the base. Use strips of black paper to make streets. Use masking tape for sidewalks and plazas around buildings. To make trees, attach wavy forms of green paper to toothpicks. Use blue construction paper for fountains (or a river). You can be as elaborate as you like, but make sure you have included the essentials for a functional neighborhood.

Skyscraper Design: A Balance of Structure & Style

When designing a skyscraper, an architect wants a building that's bold, eye-catching, and distinct in the city skyline — a unique reflection of his own creative vision. At the same time, the building needs to fit in with the other buildings in the neighborhood and make efficient use of the urban space around it.

But a design is only as good as its supporting structure. So while the architect is mostly concerned with shape, style, and design, the structural engineers are more practical in their objectives. Their foremost concern is how to build a structure for the architect's design requirements that can stand up to all the forces that will act on this huge, heavy building. And along with the forces of physics, engineers also have to take into account forces of nature, such as wind and earthquakes.

When talented architects and engineers bring their artistic visions and scientific know-how together, they create a towering building that is a dramatic visual statement, as well as a safe and strong structure. Now that's teamwork!

Wanted: Dead or Live!

All structures have to hold up their own weight, called the *dead load*, so that's the first thing engineers figure out. Dead load — the frame, sides, inside walls, floors, and windows — always stays the same, so it's easy to plan for. Add to that the *live load* — the weight of all the people, furniture, and other stuff (even the air and the water!) that goes inside the skyscraper. Because the live load continually changes, it's more difficult to figure out (but it's a fairly routine calculation for a structural engineer).

Mark and dampen sponge

Bend sponge

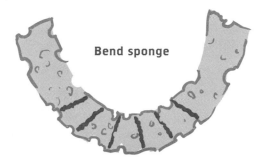

The Pull and the Push of It

Load creates two major forces that work on a skyscraper. *Compression* pushes on and squeezes parts of it. *Tension* pulls on and stretches them. It's easy to understand how the foundation, for example, would be under tremendous compression, but can parts of it be under tension at the same time? Let's see!

Try it! *Slightly dampen a sponge and mark it as shown. Bend the sponge into a U shape as if a load were on it. See what happens to the lines? On the inside of the U, they get closer because that part is being squeezed by compression. On the outside, the lines get farther apart because that part is being stretched by tension.*

Can You Carry the Load?

With all that pushing and pulling going on, how does a skyscraper stay up?

For anything to stand up, forces must be in balance. The earth is pushing up against the skyscraper while *gravity* (the force that pulls objects toward the center of the earth) is pulling it down. The skyscraper's frame has to bear the load of the building (and carry its own weight) under the tremendous forces of compression and tension. When all of these forces pushing up and pulling down are in balance, you've got a sturdy structure.

Build a frame that will stand tall and bear load. Using marshmallows as "connectors," join toothpicks together to make a square. Then use more marshmallows and toothpicks to form a cube. Continue building until you've got a toothpick tower.

Is it steady under its own dead load? What about if you put some live load, like a book, on top of it (you may need to let the marshmallows harden)?

Imagine your frame life-size and made out of steel — and you've got a real skyscraper frame. Now you know just how William Jenney (page 6) felt!

The Perfect Materials

Steel is strong *and* elastic, so it can bend and twist under the compression and tension of heavy loads without breaking. Today new kinds of super-strong steel allow skyscrapers to reach higher than ever with less material and weight.

Try it! *If you have a metal ruler at home or at school, chances are it's steel. Holding the ruler at the two ends, pull, bend, and twist it. It changes shape but doesn't break while you exert force. As soon as you remove the force, though, it returns to its original form. See how strong and elastic steel is?*

Concrete is a mix of sand, gravel, water, and cement that can be poured into wooden or steel molds called *forms* to make different shapes. The mix hardens, or *sets*, because of

a chemical reaction between the water and minerals in the cement. After it sets, it's as hard as rock and can take a lot of compression — a 3 foot (1 m) concrete cube could support 10 full jumbo jets! But unlike steel, concrete can crack and crumble under tension. To make it stronger, steel rods are put into the mold before the concrete is poured, to make *reinforced concrete*.

Try it! *You'll need a slightly damp sponge and two metal shish-kebab skewers. (Be careful of the sharp points!) It's very easy to bend the sponge, right? Now push the skewers through the sponge lengthwise. Will it bend now?*

Like this...

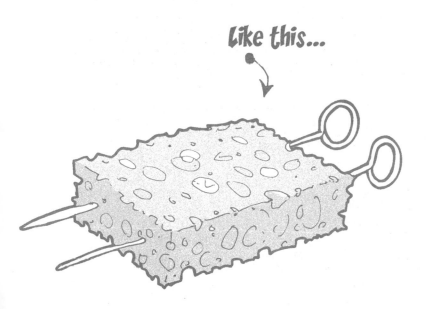

A Skyscraper from Head to Toe

A skyscraper is supported by a cagelike framework of steel beams, with a center steel or reinforced-concrete core that strengthens the building and helps hold it upright. It stands on a foundation that provides a secure footing. The walls and windows hang like a skin on the frame, protecting what's inside. Remind you of anyone? That's right — you! You can see why engineers were quick to name this building style *skeleton construction*.

Steel **BEAMS** connect horizontal girders to provide support for the concrete floors. Columns, girders, and beams have similar shapes, but girders and beams are lighter and more flexible.

The **FRAME** holds up the walls and the floors, carrying their load down to the foundation.

The **SUPERSTRUCTURE** is the part of the skyscraper that's above ground.

The **CURTAIN WALL**, or **CLADDING**, is the outside layer of the superstructure, including the windows. It hangs on the frame just like a window curtain. It doesn't support any load, but it does protect the interior of the building from the weather.

The steel **COLUMNS** are the vertical parts of the frame. They need to be very strong. Column sections may be several stories high.

Steel **GIRDERS** are the horizontal parts of the frame. They connect columns and transfer load to them.

The **CORE** runs vertically through the middle of a skyscraper like your backbone. It gives strength to the building and helps bear the load. It also provides space for elevators, stairs, and other services such as water and electricity.

The **FOUNDATION** reaches deep into the ground to give the building a firm base and keep it from tipping over.

Blowin' in the Wind

Your soda is sloshing in the cup. The hanging lamp over the table is swaying like a pendulum. You're beginning to feel a little seasick. Are you in a boat on rough seas? Nope, just on a top floor of a skyscraper on a windy day!

Wind is one of the most powerful forces acting on a tall building. Because the wind gets stronger the higher you go, the top of a skyscraper actually bends over its base in high winds. (Think of how a tree sways in the wind.) A lot of swaying can break windows, twist elevator cables, crack walls and floors, and even make people sick. Too much give, and, you guessed it, the building would blow right over!

To keep the amount of sway under control, almost a third of a modern skyscraper's steel structure serves as bracing against the force of wind. Engineers may use *supercolumns* (wider columns made of reinforced concrete) in the corners or along the sides. Sometimes the frame is attached to a concrete core. Or engineers sometimes add pieces of steel inside or outside the building that crisscross the frame like giant Xs. Chicago's 100-story John Hancock Center is an excellent example of the use of X-bracing.

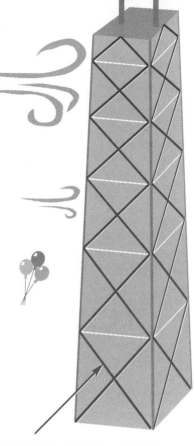

The X-shaped braces give the John Hancock Center resistance against the wind.

"On very windy days, the building sways ... the corner columns creak and groan ... and my windowpane flaps and vibrates so alarmingly that I abandon my office."
—TENANT, SEARS TOWER, CHICAGO, IL

Check That Sway!

In a properly designed skyscraper, the sway at the top in any one direction caused by wind should not be much more than the building's height in feet divided by 500 (for meters, divide by 153).

The taller of the two World Trade Center towers in New York City is 1,368 feet (421 m) and sways 3 feet (1 m) in all directions in the wind. Does the tower meet the standard building code for sway?

Answer: 1,368 feet (421 m) divided by 500 (153) = 2.7. Whew! That's close!

Wind-Test a Model Tower

Materials

- → 2 sheets of paper
- → Narrow masking tape
- → Toothpick
- → Ruler
- → Hair dryer
- → 4 strips of thin cardboard, 2" (5 cm) wide and the same length as the paper
- → Glue
- → Scissors

1 *Fold both pieces of paper in half lengthwise and tape the long sides together to make a rectangular tower. Then, set it up as shown.*

2 *Set the hair dryer on cool and hold it about 1½ feet (45 cm) away. Direct the air toward the top of the left side of the tower. Record how far the toothpick moves. This amount of sway is called* wind drift. *What else happens to the tower?*

3 *Glue the cardboard strips to the outside corners of the tower. Position the tower as before, and again test and record the wind drift. Did the corner supercolumns help resist the wind?*
4 *Add strips of masking tape to each side of the tower in Xs as shown, reposition the tower, and test again, holding the dryer the same distance away. How does this bracing compare with just the corner columns?*

Are there other ways you could make the tower stronger? Would other materials work better? Test them and see. Then remember what you've learned about wind resistance when designing your own skyscraper.

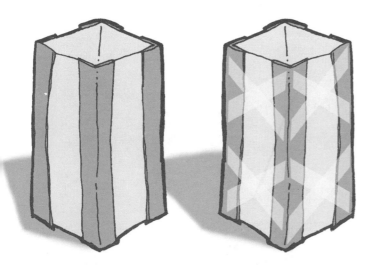

Engineering — on the Computer!

Today architects and engineers use computer programs to help determine the best structure and materials to use. The engineers enter all the details of the skyscraper's design and site into the computer. The programs analyze the forces acting on and the movements of every part of the structure to see whether — and where — it needs more bracing. These programs save both time and money. They help engineers design structures that can resist strong winds with the least amount of extra steel. And if the engineer adds more bracing, the computer makes all the new calculations.

Architects and engineers also use computer-aided design (CAD) to draw images of a skyscraper as they design it. CAD helps architects produce the thousands of blueprints (page 12) that give everyone working on the building a clear idea of what the structure will look like. CAD can even take you on a *virtual reality* tour of the proposed skyscraper by creating three-dimensional drawings!

The Citicorp Center: People Made It Happen

Many consider New York City's *Citicorp Center* the perfect example of a skyscraper that combines innovative design and carefully thought out use of public space to create a striking building that is a positive contribution to an urban neighborhood. The challenges and solutions that make up its success story are like a dramatic play unfolding, only with real-life players and situations!

Act I: An Unusual Design Team

Challenge: Citibank officials approach the owners of the 100-year-old St. Peter's Lutheran Church about building their new headquarters on a site partly occupied by the church and its grounds. The church agrees to sell all its land as long as a new church is built on the same spot. As an added challenge, Pastor Ralph Peterson wants to make sure that the area around the new church and the skyscraper is as inviting as the old church's grounds.

Solution: *Together, Pastor Peterson and the architect, **Hugh Stubbins**, persuade the bank to put a friendly plaza around its skyscraper and add a sunken garden, shops, and restaurants.*

Citicorp Center • New York, NY • 1977

Act II: A Daring Design — on Stilts!

Challenge: How will Hugh Stubbins create space underneath and around the building to accommodate this people-friendly design?

Solution: *He collaborates with the structural engineer,* **William LeMessurier***, to design something no one has seen before: They put the 59-story Citicorp Center on stilts! Four giant columns raise the 'scraper 10 stories off the ground. This approach, which sets new standards for designing spaces around skyscrapers, has been described as one of the most daring designs to be completed in the city's history!*

Citicorp Center • New York, NY • 1977

"We must develop a new generation of office buildings planned for the community and expressive of the individuals who use them."
—HUGH STUBBINS, ARCHITECT

Act III: V-Beams and Supercolumns

Challenge: The church, however, is in a corner of the site — right where a skyscraper's columns usually go. So Stubbins puts these giant columns at the *center* of each side. But much of a skyscraper's load is concentrated at the *corners.* How to carry the load?

Solution: *LeMessurier designs huge V-beams to funnel the load from the corners to the center and down into the giant columns.*

continued

Act IV: Damping the Sway

Challenge: Uh-oh! Now wind-tunnel tests of Citicorp's frame design show that the building would sway too much in the wind. How to keep the innovative structural design without using more steel bracing (which will add to the expense and change the light, airy look of the building)?

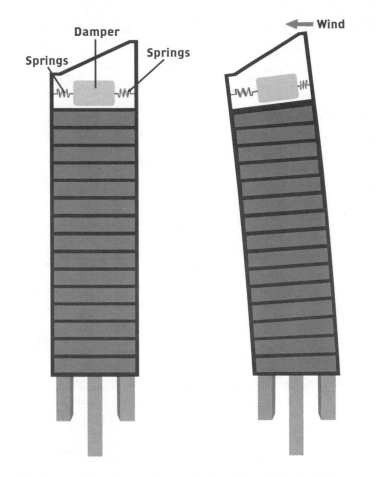

The damper is attached to opposite sides of the building by large springs and shock absorbers. Because it sits on a layer of oil, the damper hardly moves when the wind blows the building. Instead, the building slides under the damper. This causes one spring to lengthen and pull on the building and the other to shorten and push on the building. These forces immediately bring the tower back to a vertical position.

Solution: *The engineers put a tuned mass damper in a skyscraper for the first time. The damper is a 400-ton (363-t) concrete block just under the angled roof of the skyscraper. When the wind blows the building, the weight of the damper brings the building back to a vertical position. The damper acts so quickly that the people inside the tower can't even feel the building move.*

Act V: No Substitutions Allowed!

Challenge: And now for the final act in the Citicorp story. The blueprints call for welding (in *welding*, two pieces of metal are heated to join them together) the V-shaped beams to the steel frame. But the builder, trying to save money, bolts the V-beams to the frame instead. LeMessurier finds out about the substitution only *after* the skyscraper is completed. He makes new calculations and learns that if high winds hit the building at the corners, the bolted joints could break and cause the building to collapse!

Solution: *Even though his career could be ruined, LeMessurier takes responsibility for the problem, bringing it to the attention of city officials and the building's owners. He quickly designs a plan to weld special steel plates over every joint, and insists that repairs be made. Today, the Citicorp Center is safe and still in the wind. And in the end, LeMessurier is remembered for his honesty and for working so hard to fix the problem.*

The Shapes of Skyscrapers

Once you know how to build strong frames and you have the materials and technology to make them, almost any design or shape is possible. *Marina City* in Chicago — two towers that look like corncobs because the architect was tired of straight lines — are made possible by reinforced concrete. London's tallest skyscraper, the *Canary Wharf Tower*, is a big stainless steel rectangle with a pyramid on top. The *Commerzbank Tower* in Frankfurt, Germany, has a unique triangular design, with a central atrium that goes all the way to the top and elevators in the three corners rather than in the center. Another German 'scraper, the *Messeturm*, has a square base, a circular tower, and a triangle on top!

The *First Interstate Bank Tower* in Dallas, Texas, is in the shape of a giant blue-green glass crystal. Even more wild is a new hotel in the United Arab Emirates in the shape of a ship's sail. It soars more than 1,000 feet (308 m) out of the sand into the sky. New York City even has a skyscraper shaped like a lipstick!

And just as hair and clothing styles change from year to year, skyscraper styles change, too. Just look at the photos of the rectangular Reliance Building (page 8), the beautiful Chrysler Building (page 39), and the soaring Sears Tower (page 16).

Top of Lipstick Building • New York, NY • 1986

Marina City • Chicago, IL • 1964

The World's Tallest 'Scraper

One thing that never goes out of style in the world of skyscrapers is the race to build the tallest one. Chicago lost the competition early on when it restricted how tall its buildings could be. That let New York City take the lead in 1895 with the 22-story *American Surety Building*. After that it seemed that a new "tallest skyscraper" was being built in New York every couple of years. Then the Empire State Building stopped the race in 1931, keeping the title for 41 years, until the World Trade Center was built in 1972.

Then in 1974, Chicago snatched the title back with the Sears Tower, only to lose it again in 1996. This time the title went not to New York but to Kuala Lumpur, the capital of Malaysia. The taller of the two *Petronas Towers* with its tall needle-like spire is 22 feet (7 m) higher than the Sears Tower, whose TV antennae on top don't count.

Believe it or not, there is one skyscraper where the owners decided *not* to race to the sky. Toronto's 68-story *Scotia Plaza* (page 73), which opened in 1989, could have won the title of Canada's tallest if the owners had chosen to build higher than First Canadian Place. But when they asked themselves, "Why?" they couldn't come up with a good reason!

Petronas Towers • Kuala Lumpur, Malaysia • 1996

Build a Model of the Petronas Towers

The style of the Petronas Towers in Kuala Lumpur expresses the culture and heritage of Malaysia by using Islamic designs and geometric shapes. Although the towers look round from afar, they are actually eight-pointed stars made by intersecting two squares. In between the stars' points are curved walls formed by the columns underneath. A sky bridge at the 41st and 42nd floors supported by a V-shaped brace joins the two towers.

Materials

- 2 half-gallon (2 L) milk or juice cartons, with tops removed
- Scissors
- Masking tape

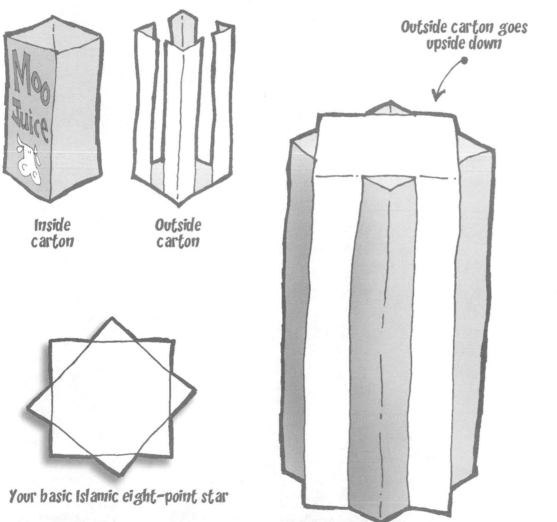

Inside carton

Outside carton

Outside carton goes upside down

Your basic Islamic eight-point star

1 Cut two slits along each side of one carton and then cut off the strips.

2 Slide the two cartons together as shown, so the corners of the inside carton stick out of the openings. When you look down at them, you should see an eight-pointed star. Tape the loose corners at the bottom.

3 Figure out a way to finish your model with more cartons. What could you use to make the curved parts of the walls? The spire? The bridge?

Detail of Woolworth Building

The Skyscraper Built with Nickels and Dimes

Could you ever save enough nickels and dimes to build a great skyscraper? Guess what? Someone did! It was Frank Woolworth, owner of the Woolworth five-and-dime department stores. In the early 1900s, he hired **Cass Gilbert** to build a great skyscraper headquarters for his company. Gilbert had studied in Europe and liked a style called *Gothic* that had been used for cathedrals during the Middle Ages.

And that's just what the *Woolworth Building* in New York City looks like. Its tall tower rises above a base like a steeple. The building is decorated inside and out with figures called *gargoyles* and other fancy carvings. One of the gargoyles is a carving of Woolworth himself, counting nickels! Another is of Gilbert looking at a model of the building. Inside, the hallways have arched ceilings in the Gothic tradition. Woolworth paid for the building — all $13.5 million of it — in cash!

Woolworth Building • New York, NY • 1913

SUPER 'SCRAPERS!

The Sneaky 'Scraper

To many people, the *Chrysler Building* in New York City is one of the most beautiful skyscrapers in the world. Its shiny spire, or crown, is decorated in a series of sunbursts with triangular windows. Originally the headquarters of the Chrysler automobile company, the building's setbacks are decorated with stylized cars, hood ornaments, and hubcaps.

It's also the sneakiest skyscraper in the competition to be the tallest. At the same time the Chrysler was going up, so was the *Bank of Manhattan Building*. At first it looked as though the bank would be taller by a mere two feet (60 cm), but the Chrysler's architect had a trick up his sleeve. He had a spire secretly assembled inside the building. (These competitions are serious!) To the surprise of just about everyone in New York City, out popped the spire after the bank was completed, crowning the Chrysler Building as the tallest skyscraper in the world — but only until the following year when the Empire State Building was completed.

What Do the People Think?

Not all new skyscraper styles are appreciated at first. Many people complained that the glass-box style was too plain and industrial-looking when it first appeared in the 1950s.

Sometimes it just takes a while for people to accept something new. When the Transamerica Pyramid (page 49) was going up, people picketed it, wearing caps in the shape of pyramids. Now it's a famous landmark in San Francisco.

But some buildings are never accepted. In a 1987 poll, New Yorkers ranked the massive *Pan Am* (now called *MetLife*) *Building,* which has blocked the view up and down one of New York City's most famous avenues since 1963, the skyscraper they'd most like to see destroyed!

Most disliked in New York City

Pan Am Building • New York, NY • 1963

Chrysler Building • New York, NY • 1930

Build the Chrysler Spire

1 *Wrap the bottle in foil and draw sunbursts and triangular windows on it to look like the crown of the Chrysler Building.*
2 *To make the pointed top: Cut the cardboard tube to the right shape, cover it in foil, and insert it into or over the neck of the bottle. Tape if needed.*
3 *Remove both ends of the box and wrap it in foil. Draw arches and put in windows so it looks like the section of the building just below the crown. Place the crown in the box and pop up the spire any time you want the tallest building!*

Materials

- ➔ Large plastic juice or soda bottle
- ➔ Aluminum foil
- ➔ Black marker
- ➔ Scissors
- ➔ Toilet-paper tube
- ➔ Tape
- ➔ Box slightly larger than the bottle

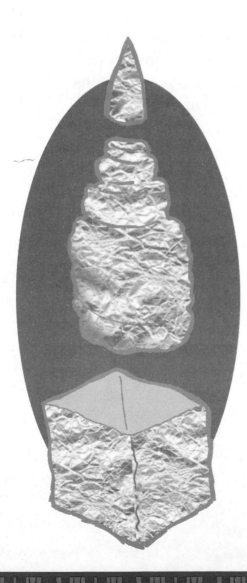

TAKE THE CHALLENGE!

Design Your Own 'Scraper

When you built your model city (pages 22–23), you created a specific site where you'd like to situate your own skyscraper. You've seen the inspired results of brilliant architects and engineers working together to create skyscrapers in all shapes and sizes. Now it's your turn to apply your creative ideas and scientific awareness, and make some preliminary design sketches.

1 *On a separate piece of paper (graph paper helps), draw an outline of the site's shape. Decide where to put the skyscraper — smack in the middle? off to one side? — and lightly sketch it in. Consider your site's surroundings and the amount of space available, if any, for parks, a plaza, walkways, and small plantings.*

2 *Next, decide how tall you'll build your skyscraper (are you going for a record-breaker?). Is your site near historic buildings or in a residential neighborhood of smaller apartment buildings? If so, the zoning laws will restrict the height of your skyscraper. How wide and deep will it need to be at the base (think back to the toothpick tower)? Now, refine your sketch from step 1 so that you have a clear drawing of your building's footprint (like your footprint, this is the shape it makes on the ground) exactly where it will sit on the site.*

How wide?

Parks?

Plantings?

Where?

Walkways?

Space?

HOW TALL?

How deep?

And a tuna room!

continued

3 Decide on the style and design. Are you going for a sleek, modern look that incorporates geometric shapes, or do you prefer a more traditional shape? How about something entirely new? Do you want your building to taper to a slender point, like the Empire State Building, or have an angled top like Citicorp Center? The indented corners of First Canadian Place in Toronto double the number of corner offices — can you think of a design feature that will bring more light into your building's interior? Sketch your design from different angles, the same way architects do.

4 Review your sketch and imagine this building on the site you chose in your model city. Does it blend into the neighborhood? Or is it out of scale with its surroundings? Do you need to revise your design? When you're satisfied with your design, save your drawing for the next challenge.

Building from the Bottom Up

Does it surprise you to learn that before you can build up, you first must build *down*? Just as your body rests firmly on your feet, a building must stand on a secure foundation. Foundations transfer all the load of a skyscraper into the ground.

The best base for a foundation is *bedrock*, the solid layer of rock that lies below the soil and clay on the surface of the earth. New York City is a great place for skyscrapers because its bedrock is easy to reach. But in some cities, the bedrock is really far down. Sometimes there's *hardpan*, a packed layer of hard clay and pieces of rock, in the way, or there may be deep or thick layers of wet clay and sand. Geotechnical engineers (pages 12 and 13) perform soil tests and search for bedrock, and the structural engineers use this information to design the proper type of foundation for the site and the architect's design. Without that specific engineering design, the building might slowly sink into the ground — or maybe even collapse!

Searching for a Solid Base

When engineers find bedrock near the surface, they've got it easy! The soil is dug out and the surface of the bedrock is leveled. To construct the *footings* that provide a solid base for the foundation, holes are drilled into the rock and then filled with concrete.

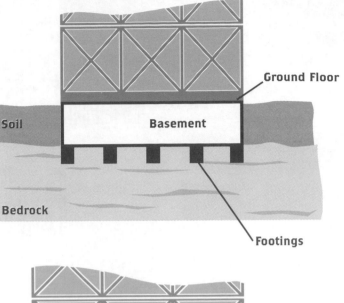

If the bedrock is deeper, engineers design *piles* as part of the foundation. These are like the roots of a tree. Using pile drivers, construction workers hammer long steel columns through the soil and clay into the bedrock. Or, they may drill deep holes through to the rock and then fill them with reinforced concrete. Piles may go down as much as one-fourth of a building's superstructure, so in a 100-story building, the piles would be dug 25 stories *downward*!

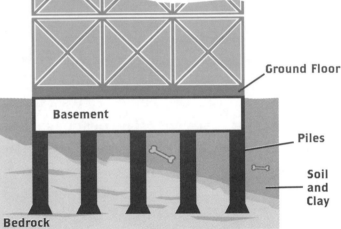

When the bedrock is too deep to reach and the ground above it is soft sand or soggy clay, one way to build a foundation is to dig out the site and pour a thick slab of concrete over it. Called a *raft*, this huge slab keeps the building from sinking the same way a raft keeps you from sinking in the water.

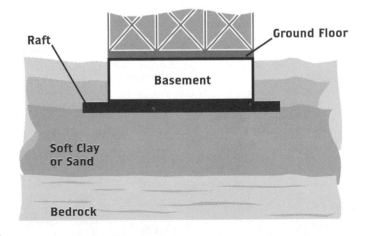

SUPER 'SCRAPERS!

Skyscrapers with Wet Feet

Some skyscrapers use a combination of foundation methods. The city of London, England, sits on layers of soggy clay and gravel that can't support the weight of a skyscraper. For the *National Westminster Tower*, 375 steel piles were driven through the clay to gravel far below. Deep trenches were dug to drain water away, and then a circular reinforced-concrete raft — as big as a soccer field — was poured on top of the piles. The skyscraper sits on top.

Deep layers of soggy clay and hardpan cover the bedrock under Chicago. To support the Sears Tower (page 16), workers dug a hole 100 feet (31 m) deep. Then they built 200 waterproof forms into the hard-pan (the ones under the tower reach the bedrock below) and filled them with concrete to make piles. The tops of the piles are connected to a huge concrete raft, which forms the lowest level of the basement. The raft and a special waterproof wall surrounding the site keep it dry.

Experiment with Rafts and Piles

Spread out a 1 inch (2.5 cm) layer of modeling clay (the soil at your foundation site). Lay a piece of cardboard on it (your raft) and put a heavy book on top (your skyscraper). Does it make a dent?

Now stand a couple of toothpicks (piles) in the clay and try to rest the book on them. Can't do it? Try many toothpicks spread out all over the clay.

With either a raft or many piles, you spread out the book's weight (the load) and supported it. All foundations work just that way, by spreading the compression force of a building over a large area.

SKYSCRAPER

LOAD

SOIL

RAFT

PILES

The Foundation Phase: Who Does What

If you like big, powerful machines, you'll love this part of building a skyscraper! Lots of equipment and many people work together to dig such an enormous hole and build the huge foundation. The builder hires SUBCONTRACTORS that specialize in digging sites and putting in foundations. The sub-contractors hire the WORKERS who operate the equipment and do the work.

3 A pile driver hammers piles through the remaining soil into the bedrock below. Or, an *auger* (or rotary drill) attached to a crane, drills holes. Then, the workers put steel columns into the holes and pour concrete around them.

CAN YOU DIG IT?

1 Sometimes old buildings on the site have to be demolished before digging can begin. Workers use dynamite to blow up the buildings or use machines like wrecking cranes to knock them down. Bulldozers and dump trucks clear away the rubble.

2 After surveyors mark the location of the foundation, workers come in with excavators and backhoes to dig the hole. Hydraulic hammers break up big rocks. Cranes remove heavy rock or pieces of the old building's basement.

NELS CONS

4 To make pile caps, concrete is poured into *forms* (wooden frames that hold the concrete while it hardens) on top of each pile. Metal rods called anchor bolts stick up out of the tops of the caps. Later on, these rods are bolted to the steel frame, connecting the foundation to the superstructure.

5 Finally, cement mixers stream onto the site to pour the slab of concrete that covers the piles. The slab becomes the lowest floor of the basement. The workers also pour the foundation walls, which become the walls of the skyscraper's basement.

Search for Bedrock

Test these four construction sites to determine what type of foundation you'll need for each one.

Materials

- → 4 small identical plastic containers or cups
- → Marker
- → Piece of wood that fits inside a container or cup
- → Soil and sand
- → Ruler
- → Pencil and paper
- → Tape
- → Toilet-paper tube
- → 5 identical blocks
- → Flathead nails
- → Section of stiff cardboard

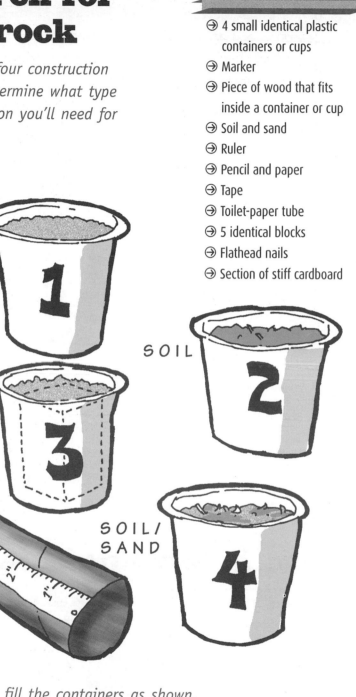

SAND — 1
SOIL — 2
SAND/WOOD — 3
SOIL/SAND — 4

1 *Label and fill the containers as shown.*

2 *Mark a scale in $^1/_8$ inch (3 mm) increments on a piece of tape and attach it to the tube.*

continued

3 *Draw this table on the paper to record your data. Gently place the tube in container #1. Place one block on the tube and record the distance the tube sinks. Add another block and record the distance. Continue until all five blocks are on the tube. Remove the blocks and press on the tube. If the tube doesn't go down any farther, put a check mark by container #1 in your table. You're at or near the bedrock. If the tube sinks more, put an X in that column. To "build" a five-block tower on this site, it's going to be a little more challenging to design a foundation that reaches bedrock. Repeat for each container, recording all results in the table.*

Now, be an engineer!

- Which site has bedrock closest to the surface? Would this be a good place to excavate and pour footings for the foundation base?
- Which site would provide the least amount of support for a building? Would piles or a raft work best here?
- Which containers would need piles to reach bedrock? Will you have to excavate as well? (Consider the length of the nails you have for piles.)

Test your conclusions, using nail "piles" or a cardboard "raft" where you think you need them. As on a real construction site, there may be more than one approach, but if the load no longer sinks, you've got a good foundation!

Rialto Towers • Melbourne, Australia • 1985

SUPER 'SCRAPERS!

A Quake-Proof Pyramid

San Francisco is known for its cable cars, the Golden Gate Bridge, and ... earthquakes. So when you build a skyscraper there, you'd better build it strong and make it earthquake-proof.

At 48 stories and topped with a 212 foot (65 m) spire covered with aluminum panels, the *Transamerica Pyramid* is San Francisco's tallest building. The foundation rests on bedrock. When earthquakes shake the soft soil around the foundation, it doesn't move much. But even little vibrations can become more powerful as they move up into the superstructure. To prevent that, there are huge shock absorbers between the foundation and the frame. In addition, the steel frame is flexible so it also absorbs vibrations. Finally, the glass windows are set in reinforced-concrete panels, so the cladding is extra-strong as well.

SUPER 'SCRAPERS!

A Sturdy 'Scraper Down Under

Australia's tallest 'scraper, the *Rialto Towers* in Melbourne, is made of reinforced concrete and glass. It sits on top of 75 concrete supports, called *caissons,* that are attached to bedrock. After an earthquake in Newcastle, Australia, in 1989, the Rialto was put through an earthquake analysis and passed with flying colors!

Transamerica Pyramid •
San Francisco, CA • 1972

TAKE THE CHALLENGE!

Design and Build Your Skyscraper's Foundation

Materials

- ➔ Plastic container, 6" (15 cm) high and slightly larger than the base of your skyscraper as drawn in your design
- ➔ Sand and soil to fill the container
- ➔ 3" or 4" (75- or 100-mm) flathead nails, 10 to 15
- ➔ 2 pieces of stiff cardboard that fit in the container
- ➔ Tape

You just received the results on the soil tests from your site. Good news! The bedrock is very close to the surface and the soil is dry and sandy. But the geotechnical engineer reminds you that earthquakes are a concern in this area.

Review Searching for a Solid Base (page 44) before you begin designing your foundation. Think about your results from Search for Bedrock (page 47) to determine what materials you will need: a slab of clay for a raft? Cardboard tubes for footings? Nails for piles? And consider the soil conditions of the Super 'Scrapers in this chapter.

If you decided that because of the earthquake threat, concrete footings wouldn't anchor the building securely enough and you'd need to use piles, you'd make a great structural engineer! Now you're ready to build your foundation.

Fill the container with 2 inches (5 cm) of soil and pack it down. Add sand so the height of the sand and soil is equal to the length of the nails.

Poke the nails through one piece of cardboard in a pattern similar to the one shown. Tape the second piece of cardboard on top, covering the nail heads. The nails are the piles. Push them down through the sand and soil so the cardboard rests on top of the sand.

You now have a sturdy pile foundation, and a basement floor with walls all ready for your skyscraper! Save it for the framing challenge in the next chapter.

The Skeleton Rises

Once the foundation is complete, the massive steel frame rises quickly into the sky. Just how do those thousands of steel columns, girders, and beams all end up in exactly the right place? If you've ever built a model airplane or some other structure from a kit where all the pieces and instructions are coded, then you know exactly what it's like to build a skyscraper frame. If you follow the order of the instructions and match the codes on the pieces, your airplane looks great! If you don't, watch out. The whole thing may fall apart!

With skyscrapers, builders use an amazing system of organization that starts by labeling every one of those pieces of steel on the building's blueprints with a special code, just like in your model kits. The blueprints indicate the size and shape of each piece — even where the holes for bolting the pieces together should be placed! The pieces are also labeled with their special code.

Steelyard • Providence, RI • 2001

The Framing Phase: Who Does What

Putting up the frame — seeing the skeleton grow by leaps and bounds almost daily — is the most exciting time in the building of a skyscraper!

If you have a problem or question on the job site, you'll need to find "the Clerk of the Works." Usually a **STRUCTURAL ENGINEER**, this person is on site throughout the construction of the building. He or she makes sure the frame is being built according to the plans and coordinates with the architect, other engineers, city officials, and various subcontractors so the work moves quickly and smoothly along.

The **IRONWORKERS** climb all over the frame as if it were a giant jungle gym, joining sections of steel together according to the plans. The joints between the sections must be just as strong as the sections themselves. Ironworkers and **WELDERS** bolt and weld the sections together.

CRANE OPERATORS climb into the cabs of mobile cranes to lift material off the trucks and set it near where it will be installed. They operate tower cranes to swing columns and beams up to the level where they are needed.

Workers also get materials to upper floors using hoists, boxlike cages that move up and down the outside of the building like elevators.

WORKERS *place*, or pour, the concrete for floors (and for columns that aren't steel).

Is that gum?

The **ARCHITECT** and a **CITY INSPECTOR** visit the site regularly to make sure the framing is being done correctly. **SAFETY ENGINEERS** and **INSPECTORS** from OSHA (Occupational Safety and Health Administration) also visit the site, making sure the general contractor is following all health and safety requirements as prescribed by federal law.

"Where Do You Want These Girders?"

Crane operators have a *huge* responsibility. They have the final say over how much can be lifted and how high it can go. If they lift too much, the crane could break and the load could fall on someone below. But even really loud shouting can't be heard above the constant noise and commotion of a construction site and bad weather can make it impossible to see. So he knows where to "land iron," or place his load, the crane operator communicates with a worker on the ground via radio. When visibility is good, they use hand signals.

Try it! *Load up a friend with a stack of books. Now, direct her where to "land" it using these hand signals! Remember, no words!*

| "Boom up!" | "Hoist!" | "Lower!" | "Swing!" |

"It usually takes about a year. Maybe your hands are sweating, you're shaking, you've got a lump in your stomach. But if it's in you to do the work, that'll go away, and you'll start to feel comfortable. You can't do the work with one hand holding on all the time. You'll just end up getting hurt or hurting somebody else."
— *JACK DOYLE, IRONWORKER*

Columns, Beams, and Girders

Columns, which stand in a vertical position, have an H shape. The wide sides of the H, or *flanges*, keep the columns from buckling, or bending, as they are compressed by the heavy load above them. Because columns for the lower floors carry more load, they are usually thicker and stronger than the ones on upper floors.

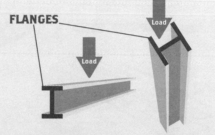

FLANGES Load Load

Most girders and floor beams have an I shape with narrow flanges. They lie horizontally in the frame, so they carry weight along their length. They're squeezed along the top and stretched along the bottom, so although they need to be lighter than columns (to reduce the load they create), they still need to be strong under both compression and tension.

Build a Two-Story Frame

See how columns and girders create a freestanding framework that can support a floor. (To make it easier, you'll use beams with the same-sized flanges for both columns and girders.)

Materials

- 20 strips of paper, 2" x 11" (6 x 28 cm)
- Ruler
- Pencil
- Glue
- Tape
- Scissors
- 2 rectangular pieces of cardboard

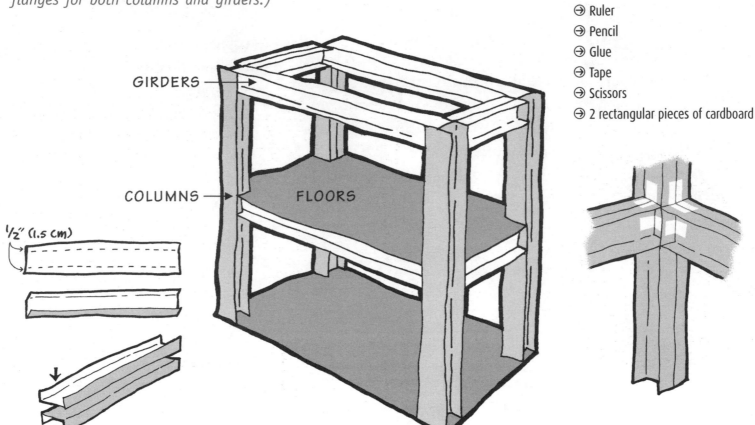

GIRDERS

COLUMNS

FLOORS

½" (1.5 cm)

1 On each strip, draw lines as shown. Fold each strip along those lines.

2 Glue pairs of folded strips together back-to-back to make 10 beams. Place a strip of tape along the top and bottom flanges. Cut two of these long beams in half to make four short ones.

3 Position four long beams in a rectangle on the cardboard "foundation" and tape these columns in place. The remaining beams are the girders. Tape the long girders on the sides and the short girders on the ends to make a frame.

4 Place the other piece of cardboard on the girders for the middle floor.

> "You get the worst of it up here. In the winter, the beams get real cold and you freeze. In the summer, the sun beats off the metal decking, and it's like a microwave oven. The beams get hot. Real hot."
> —JOE GAFFNEY, IRONWORKER FOR 13 YEARS

Build a Tower Crane

Tower cranes are the most important machines involved in raising a skyscraper's skeleton. Cranes use simple machines like pulleys and counterweights to lift and move heavy loads. Make one to see how it works!

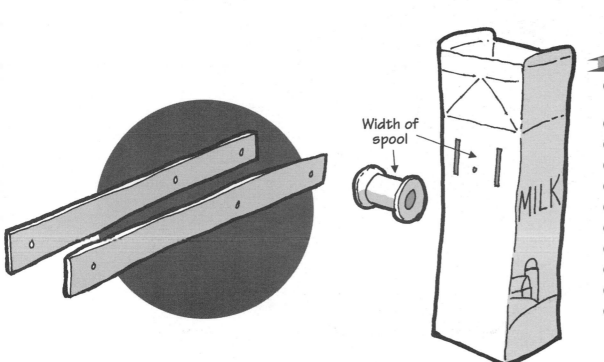

Width of spool

Materials

- ➔ 2 strips of cardboard, 1 1/2" x 12" (3.5 x 30 cm), plus another small section
- ➔ Hole punch
- ➔ Milk or juice carton, 1 qt (1 L)
- ➔ 2 empty thread spools, same size
- ➔ 2 drinking straws
- ➔ Pencil
- ➔ String, about 4' (1.2 m)
- ➔ Metal hook
- ➔ Scissors
- ➔ Masking tape
- ➔ Nuts and washers

1 *Use the cardboard strips to make the crane's jib (or boom). Punch three holes in both strips as shown, making sure the holes line up.*

2 *The carton will serve as the crane's climbing frame and operator's cab. Open the top of the carton. Cut two slits on opposite sides for the cardboard strips to slide through. The distance between the slits should equal the width of the spool. On one side, poke a small hole between the slits.*

3 *Slide the cardboard strips (the jib) through the slits and line up the holes. Position the middle holes inside the carton so the jib has one long arm and one short arm. Tape a small piece of cardboard between the strips at each end to make them sturdier. Now, poke holes in the carton that line up with the jib's middle holes. Slide a piece of straw through the carton and the jib's middle holes.*

continued

4 *Use a piece of straw to position a spool between the holes at the end of the long arm. Slide the pencil through the holes at the end of the short arm.*

5 *Tape the carton to the table. Place the string over the jib spool. Then thread it through the hole between the slits, under the straw, and out of the top of the carton.*

Punch holes at the top of the carton and position a spool there. Bring the string up over this spool and out of the carton. Tie the end of the string to the pencil and twist it to wind up the string.

6 *Tie the hook to the end of the string. Hang metal nuts and washers from the hook and try lifting the load by twisting the*

pencil. Both spools should move freely on the straws. If the straws move, too, tape around the holes.

Try it! *A real crane uses counter-weights to keep from toppling over. Remove the tape attaching your crane to the table. Holding your crane, hang a load from the hook. Place washers on the pencil until the load is balanced and the crane can stand by itself.*

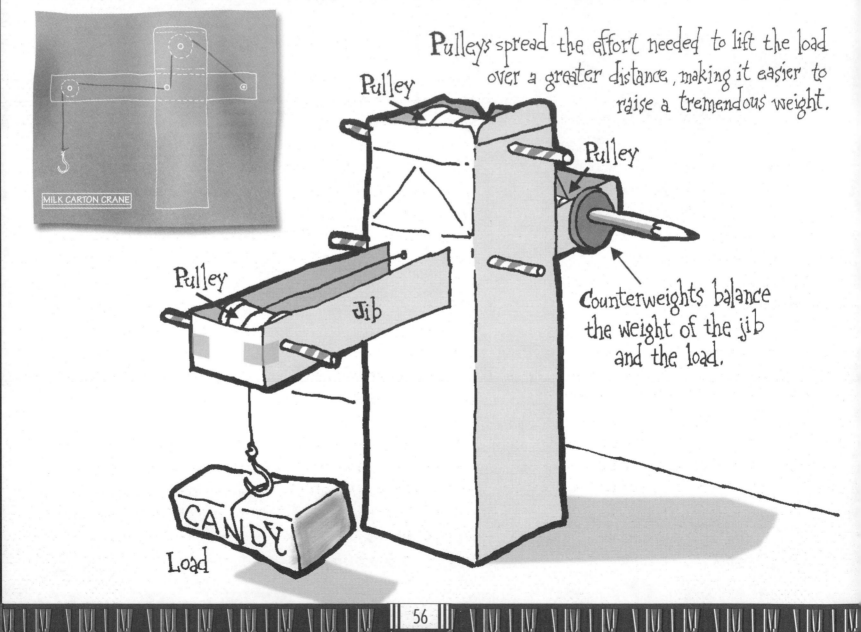

MILK CARTON CRANE

Pulleys spread the effort needed to lift the load over a greater distance, making it easier to raise a tremendous weight.

Pulley

Pulley

Pulley

Jib

Counterweights balance the weight of the jib and the load.

CANDY

Load

How Tower Cranes Climb

A tower crane starts out on the ground with its frame, cab, and jib on a base that is usually attached to the foundation. Inside the frame is a hydraulic jack, similar to the jack that lifts up a car at a service station but much more powerful. As the jack lifts the cab, new sections are added to the crane's frame to make the crane grow.

But the crane can't grow as tall as a skyscraper frame. To rise higher, it climbs right up the building. The crane is lifted off the base to a new level where it's bolted onto the skyscraper's frame. And so it goes, up and up, until it reaches the top of the skyscraper.

The Riveting Gang

On older skyscrapers like the Empire State Building, the columns and girders were fastened together by special bolts called *rivets* by workers called *riveters*, who worked in groups, or gangs, of four. The noise of metal hitting metal was ear shattering, even to onlookers on the ground far below, who could see sparks fly as the hot rivet fused with the steel pieces.

The *heater's job* was to get the rivets red-hot in a forge, then pick one up with long tongs, and sling it 50 feet (15 m) or so up to the *catcher*.

The catcher caught the rivet in a tin can, picked it up with tongs, and stuck it into one of the holes in the steel connecting plate.

As the *bucker-up* propped up the rivet with a special tool, the *gunman* hammered the rivet in place with an air gun.

Each riveting gang trained together as closely as a trapeze act in a circus. Their jobs were extremely danger-ous and their lives depended on their skill, strength, and teamwork. In bad weather, riveters refused to work. Can you blame them? Imagine trying to cling to a girder 80 stories high in the wind or when it was so cold your hands were numb.

Racing Riveters!

Riveting gangs often competed to see which team could go faster. Gather enough friends to make up two teams of four players each, and see which one finishes first with the most "rivets" in rings to win the race!

Materials

→ At least 10 bean bags or other soft, small toys
→ Equal number of paper rings
→ 2 buckets
→ 2 pairs of tongs
→ 2 sticks

Heater

Catcher

Bucker-up

Gunman

Divide the bean bags (the rivets) and the rings (the holes in the steel plates) evenly between the teams. The teams start at the same time.

1 *The heater picks up a bean bag with the tongs and tosses it to the catcher, who must catch it in the bucket.*

2 *The catcher uses the tongs to put the "rivet" inside a ring.*

3 *As the bucker-up touches the "rivet" with the stick, the gunman slaps it and then calls to the heater to throw another one.*

4 *If the catcher misses the "rivet," the heater throws another one and play continues. Missed "rivets" don't count. The team with the most "rivets" in wins.*

The Frame Gallery

The Empire State Building (page 14) is an example of the classic steel frame. It looks like a jungle gym with a steel core in the middle. Columns are on the inside as well as the outside, so the floor space between the core and the walls is interrupted.

In the 1960s, a new way of putting a frame together was developed that eliminated the interior columns and made new heights possible with less steel.

Structural engineer **Fazlur Khan**, who was born in Bangladesh, designed the *tube frame*, first used in Chicago's John Hancock Center. It cut in half the amount of steel normally required for a building of this height!

Khan used this frame again for the two towers of the World Trade Center. Each tower is like a huge, square tube with another tube, the core, in the middle. Closely spaced steel columns make up the exterior. Floor beams connect these columns to the steel core.

With the Sears Tower (page 16), Khan took the tube frame one step further. Or is it nine steps further? After all, it's simply a bundle of nine square tube frames of different heights in a tic-tac-toe arrangement. Inside walls are shared by neighboring tubes.

"I strive for structural simplicity ... the technical man mustn't be lost in his own technology."
— *FAZLUR KHAN, STRUCTURAL ENGINEER*

Cross-section view of three different types of frames

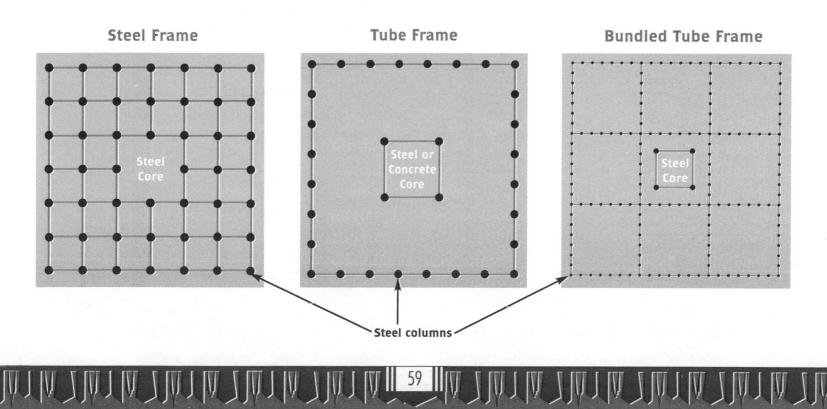

Steel Frame — Steel Core

Tube Frame — Steel or Concrete Core

Bundled Tube Frame — Steel Core

Steel columns

SUPER 'SCRAPERS!

A Hurricane-Proof 'Scraper

Originally, concrete was only used for low or medium-sized skyscrapers because it is so heavy. But with today's new lighter but stronger kind of concrete and new construction methods, even very tall concrete buildings are now possible.

China's *Jin Mao Tower* in Shanghai, the fourth tallest skyscraper in the world, rests on sandy soil with no bedrock in an area known for *typhoons* (tropical hurricanes) and earthquakes. The advanced design that makes it possible includes a reinforced concrete core and steel and concrete supercolumns.

In the Chinese culture, eight is a lucky number, which makes the Jin Mao Tower very lucky indeed! The segments of the building are divided into eight levels. There are also eight supercolumns of concrete and eight of steel to fortify the building against typhoons and earthquakes. And best of all, the crown reaches the sky at the 88th floor!

"Topping Out"

When the tower crane operator hoists the last beam to the top and the ironworkers attach it, everyone celebrates. Sometimes the workers raise a flag or a small fir tree on the top when they reach the summit. The architects and owners may join the workers in the party.

When the Sears Tower topped out, the "Tower Bums," a band formed by electrical workers, sang a song they had written. It began, "She towers so high, just scraping the sky, she's the tallest rock." The last beam in the Tower was special, too. More than 12,000 workers, Sears employees, and citizens of Chicago signed their names on the beam before it went up.

TAKE THE CHALLENGE!

Design and Build A Skyscraper Frame

Now your skyscraper will really start to take shape! Using your design sketches (pages 41–42) as reference, decide what kind of frame will be best. Here's what you need to consider:

1 Does your building have a traditional shape that is suited to the classic jungle-gym-style frame? Or have you designed a super-tall structure that you hope will take the title of "world's tallest?" Maybe you designed a building with a lot of setbacks — your frame will need to reflect that (think of the Sears Tower, page 16).

2 Uh-oh! Wind-tunnel tests of a model of your design have just come in from the structural engineer, indicating that excessive sway is a concern.

Where will you need supercolumns?

3 Remember, too, that the frame will determine the final shape of your skyscraper. If you sketched a Citicorp Center–style top (page 32), the frame design will need to show that.

4 Decide how far apart each floor should be and how many floors will be needed to reach the height you want. Now, draw a floor plan that shows the position of all the supercolumns, columns, and girders. Then, determine the length and number of columns and girders you will need.

continued

Now, following your floor plan, you're ready to build your skyscraper's frame on your foundation (page 50)!

Materials

- Old newspaper or magazine pages
- Narrow masking tape
- Scissors
- Ruler
- Fan or hair dryer

1 *Roll the paper to make enough columns and girders for the first couple of floors. Tape the edges of the rolls so they don't unravel. Make thicker rolls for supercolumns.*

2 *Tape columns and supercolumns to the cardboard top of your foundation according to their position in your floor plan. They should be right up against the basement walls. Now, connect the girders to the columns. It helps to slit the ends of girders and wrap the flaps around a column to tape them in place.*

3 *Keep connecting columns and girders. Use the ruler to check the distance between floors before taping girders. To make columns taller, tape two rolled pieces end-to-end. Overlapping them a bit will make them stronger.*

4 *Keep checking your design drawing as you build up. Remember to put in any setbacks or different shapes. When the last beam is in place, have a "topping out" party. You deserve it!*

5 *Using a fan or hair dryer, test your skyscraper in the wind. Does it need additional bracing?*

SAND
SOIL

Finishing Touches

Once the frame of a skyscraper is underway, the building is buzzing with activity — from top to bottom, inside *and* out. As soon as each floor of the frame is built, more workers arrive to begin the finishing work. They pour concrete floors and install plumbing pipes and electrical wires. Stairs are built and elevators are installed inside the core. On the outside, more workers hang the curtain walls (page 74) and put in the windows so the inside walls can be built, plastered, and painted. On a really big skyscraper, workers are already installing carpeting, light fixtures, and plumbing fixtures while the frame is being finished many stories above. There may be as many as 1,000 workers on the site on a single day, all getting the skyscraper ready for its occupants.

"Most of the public thinks a building like this just happens,
it jumps up out of the ground. Well, nothing could be further
from the truth. It takes a lot of work, thousands and
thousands of man-hours, maybe a million, to construct
a building like this. You'd be surprised!"
—CONSTRUCTION WORKER
ON A HIGH-RISE OFFICE BUILDING

A Day in the Life of an Almost Skyscraper
The Finishing Phase: Who Does What

Imagine the busy scene at a skyscraper's construction site on just a single day.

A **GENERAL CONTRACTOR** coordinates all the many different subcontractors that are needed on the site all at the same time.

The **SAFETY ENGINEER** visits the site to check on the working conditions of the hundreds of people on the job.

As a **CRANE OPERATOR** lifts girders to steelworkers on the 60th story, workers pour and finish concrete floors over the steel decking on the 57th.

Workers fireproof the frame on the 55th floor.

A few floors below, **ELECTRICIANS** install wiring, **TECHNICIANS** put in heating and air-conditioning ducts, and **PLUMBERS** fit pipes together. Soon the space under the floors becomes crisscrossed with pipes and ducts. A **CITY INSPECTOR** shows up to check the wiring and plumbing.

MECHANICAL CREWS begin installing elevators in the core. Workers connect the wiring, pipes, and ducts from each floor to the main ones that run through the core. Eventually, everything will be connected to the service centers in the basement and elsewhere.

On huge scaffolds hanging from the frame at the 50th story, workers hang the cladding (page 74) that will cover the outside of the skyscraper, forming the curtain wall.

A huge window dangles from a crane as GLAZIERS struggle to set it in place.

An ARCHITECT visits the site to make sure the plans for the curtain's design are being followed correctly.

On the 45th floor, already closed in by its curtain wall, armies of finishing workers like

CARPENTER, PLASTERERS, and PLUMBERS turn the empty space into hallways, rooms, closets, and bathrooms.

In an office building, an INTERIOR ARCHITECT or designer determines each floor's layout based on the tenant's needs.

On the lower floors, INTERIOR DECORATORS help tenants make decisions about colors and carpets as still more workers paint, hang wallpaper, lay carpets, install lighting fixtures, and put on all the other finishing touches.

Don't Splash in These Puddles!

If you liked playing with squishy mud when you were younger, you'd love making concrete floors! After carpenters build forms and concrete is poured, **cement puddlers** wade right into the wet goo to spread it out. Then **cement masons** push long *bull floats* over the surface to smooth it. They have to move quickly before the concrete hardens!

Lay a "Concrete Floor"

It's your turn to be a cement mason! See how smooth you can get this floor.

Note: *Ask an adult for help when boiling water and cooking on the stove.*

Materials

- ⊕ Tea kettle
- ⊕ Double boiler or small pot that will fit in a larger pot of water
- ⊕ 1 cup (250 ml) sand
- ⊕ $^1/_2$ cup (125 ml) cornstarch
- ⊕ Glue
- ⊕ 2 Popsicle sticks
- ⊕ Cookie sheet
- ⊕ Aluminum foil

1 *Boil water in the kettle and in the bottom (larger) pot of the double boiler (with grown-up help). Meanwhile, away from the stove, mix the sand and cornstarch in the top (smaller) pot.*

2 *When both the kettle and the bottom pot are boiling, ask your adult helper to add $^1/_2$ cup (125 ml) of the kettle's boiling water to the mixture. Set the small pot on top of the larger pot and stir the mixture. Stop when it gets thick. (If it gets too thick, add a bit more hot water.) Let it cool until you can touch it.*

3 *Glue the Popsicle sticks together to form a T for a bull float. Cover the cookie sheet with foil. Spread the mixture over the foil and use the bull float to smooth it out. Put it in the oven at a low temperature (275°F/140°C) until it dries.*

Fireproofing the Frame

Steel doesn't actually burn, but the high temperatures of a fire can cause it to buckle. There are several ways to protect the columns, girders, and floor beams from this intense heat. Workers sometimes spray or paint them with special fireproof material. Or, workers wrap each steel section in a blanket made of special fireproof fibers, attaching it with a stainless steel netting. Then they cover the whole section in *turkey wrap*, a special fire-resistant aluminum foil. Another way to protect the steel frame is to completely cover each piece with concrete.

Turkey Wrap, Not turkey Rap...

Fire Safety in a Skyscraper

Fire in any building is frightening, but in a skyscraper, it can be terrifying. Consider that a 100-foot (30 m) hook and ladder truck would only reach the 5th or 6th floor — and you could be 70 stories off the ground!

To protect the hundreds of people in a skyscraper at any one time, many fire safety measures are required by law. As soon as smoke sensors detect smoke, they

Water sprinkler

automatically sound alarms and turn on water sprinklers set in the ceilings all around the skyscraper. A computer directs the air-handling units and fans to

start pushing air out of the building to get rid of the smoke.

Escape routes must be clearly marked and during emergencies, security personnel are sent to each floor to guide people out of the building. Some very tall buildings have helicopter landing pads on their roofs so people on the upper floors can escape more quickly that way instead of making their way down to the ground.

Map Out the Services

Investigate how services like electricity and water come into your home. Then, imagine efficiently organizing those services (and more!) for an 80-story building!

Materials

→ Large cardboard box lid with sides
→ Paper
→ Scissors
→ Colored pencils
→ Tape or glue
→ Colored thread
→ String
→ Drinking straws
→ Cardboard

1 *Trim the paper to fit the box lid. Sketch the layout of the rooms on the first floor of your home on the paper. Note the position of electrical outlets, heating or cooling registers, and sinks and toilets. These things tell you where plumbing, heating, and electrical services end.*

2 *Ask an adult to help you figure out where the electrical wiring, heating or cooling ducts, and pipes that lead to those things come from. They are hidden behind walls and under floors. Using different colors for the three services, draw the paths of the wires, ducts, and pipes on your sketch.*

3 *Again with an adult, find the main electrical box, furnace or air-conditioning unit, and the water tank (you'll probably have to explore the basement).*

4 *Glue the layout to the top of the lid. On the layout, cut and tape thin strips of cardboard to build walls between the rooms. Using thread for electrical wiring, string for pipes, and straws for ducts, install these services according to your sketch, connecting*

them to their sources. If any of them continue into the basement (the other side of the lid), poke holes in the lid and thread them through. Tape or glue them in place.

5 *Now look at the layout of the rooms and the positions of the wires, pipes, and ducts. Are they efficiently organized? For example, do all the pipes take the shortest, most direct route to the water source? It uses less materials and costs less that way.*

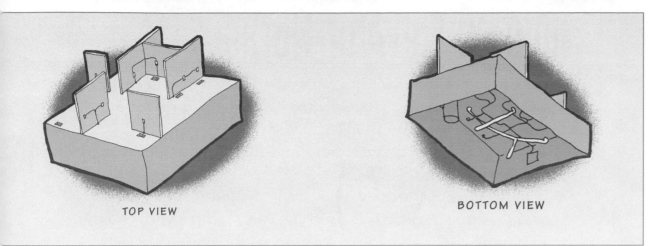

TOP VIEW   BOTTOM VIEW

"The Observation Deck, Please"

Air, electricity, and water aren't the only things that need to move efficiently throughout a large building — people do, too! The thousands of people inside skyscrapers every day want to get where they are going quickly and easily. Put in too few elevators, and you'll have impatient crowds waiting on each floor to get on board. But elevators take up lots of space, so architects also try to keep the number of elevator shafts to a minimum.

To solve this, very tall buildings are often divided into sections and have two kinds of elevators. Climb aboard an express elevator on the ground floor and you're whizzed up to the section that includes your floor. Doors open, you get off, and switch to a local elevator to get to your exact floor. First Canadian Place took another approach: It uses 32 double-decker elevators, which stop at two floors at the same time. This halves the number of shafts the building needs to get people to all of its 72 floors. Think of all the space that saves!

Japan's tallest building, the *Landmark Tower* in Yokohama, has the world's fastest elevators at 2,460 feet (757 m) per minute. That's like traveling 28 mph (45 kph) in a car. In about 40 seconds, they whiz you to the observation deck on the 69th floor for a beautiful view of snow-covered Mount Fuji.

Express elevators   **Local elevators**

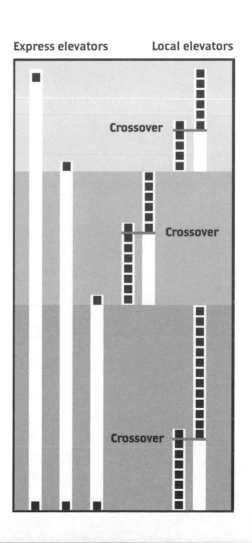

Crossover

Crossover

Crossover

Elisha Otis and the Passenger Elevator

Born in 1811 in Vermont, **Elisha Otis** liked to tinker with machines as a boy. When he grew up, he started an elevator company. Simple hoists had been used for lifting heavy freight for many centuries. What Otis invented was a safety brake: If the elevator's cable broke, the spring would straighten and catch the toothed rail on the walls of the elevator shaft. Notches on the walls caught the bars and stopped the elevator from falling. And so the passenger elevator was born.

Try it! Next time you're in an elevator, look at the name of the elevator company. More often than not, it will say Otis Elevator Company.

How an Elevator Works

An elevator rides on *rails*, like railroad tracks, inside a *shaft* in the skyscraper's core. The elevator *car* hangs on *cables* attached to a pulley-like device called a *drive sheave*.

An *electric motor* turns the *pulley*, making the elevator move up or down.

The other ends of the cables are attached to a *counterweight* that rides on its own rails behind the car. It works with the motor to move the car.

All elevator cars are equipped with *safety brakes* in case the cables break.

Spring   **Cable**

A simple elevator safety brake

Elisha Otis demonstrates the safety brake that made the passenger elevator possible.

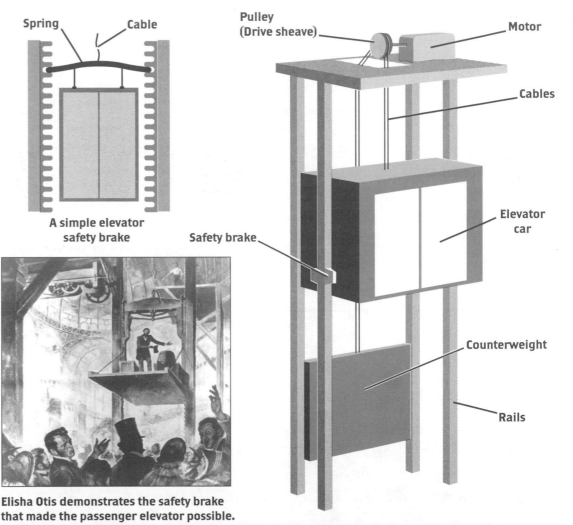

Pulley (Drive sheave)   **Motor**

Cables

Safety brake

Elevator car

Counterweight

Rails

Build an Elevator

Put the simple principles of counterweights and pulleys that you used for your tower crane (pages 55–56) to use again to make this working elevator!

Materials

- Small cardboard box, open on one side
- Ruler
- Pencil
- Poster board
- Scissors
- Tape
- String
- Large empty thread spool
- Washers
- Hole punch

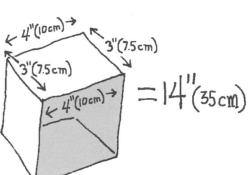

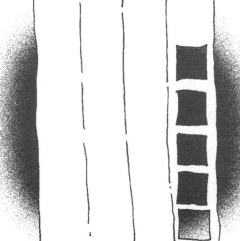

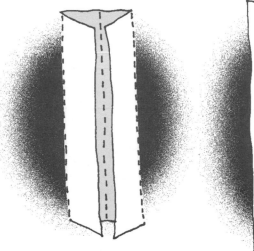

To make the shaft:

1 Measure each side of the box and add up the measurements. Add 1 inch (2.5 cm) to the total and mark that measurement on the poster board as shown. Cut off that section.

2 Fold the measured piece in half lengthwise. Open it and fold the edges in to the center fold. Open the piece.

3 Cut a piece of poster board that's 1 inch (2.5 cm) shorter and 1 inch (2.5 cm) narrower than the larger side of the box. Trace around

it several times along one side of the poster board, separating each tracing by about 1 inch (2.5 cm). Cut them out (you may need some adult help here). These are the elevator doors on different floors.

4 Fold the poster board to form a long square tube (the shaft) and tape the edges together.

5 Cut a strip of poster board that's a little narrower than the shaft and 3 inches (2.5 cm) shorter. Tape it inside the shaft near the back (opposite the cutout doors) so it's flush with the bottom. This strip will separate the car and the counterweight.

 continued

To make the car:

If necessary, trim the box so it fits inside the shaft. Cut a piece of string (the elevator cable) that's about one and a half times as long as the shaft. Attach one end of the string to the washers (the counterweight). Attach the other end to the top of the box.

SIDE
VIEW

To assemble the elevator:

1 *Drop the car into the front section of the shaft so it rests on the ground and drape the string and washers over the top of the shaft.*

2 *Punch one hole on each side of the shaft at the top just above the inside strip. Use a pencil to position the spool (the drive sheave). The spool must fit tightly on the pencil (wrap tape around it if necessary). Wrap the string around the spool a few times and then drop the washers behind the strip. Turn the pencil to lift and lower the elevator car.*

Putting on the Skin

Choosing an exterior for a skyscraper is a little like deciding what to wear — you want to look good, but you also need to dress appropriately for the occasion. It wouldn't do to go to a fancy wedding in jeans and a T-shirt or to a picnic on the beach in a suit. A skyscraper also needs to look good and fit in, so the architect chooses a material for the cladding that will fit the design of the skyscraper and its surroundings.

- **Masonry** usually makes a building look warmer and more inviting. Thin sheets of stone like granite, limestone, marble, and brick provide texture and pretty colors.

- **Metal** looks sleek and modern. Aluminum is cheap and easy to shape, while stainless steel resists weather well but is very expensive.

- **Glass**, which can be clear, tinted, or mirrored, also has a very modern look.

Combining materials makes a building more interesting. Vertical strips of stainless steel run along the limestone exterior of the Empire State Building. They look like ribbons reaching for the sky and make the building seem even taller. Toronto's Scotia Plaza (page 36) combines red granite with reflective glass cladding for a very striking look. *One Liberty Place*, the tallest building in Philadelphia, starts off at the base clad in granite. As its height increases, glass gradually replaces the stone. The pyramid top is all glass.

The designers of the Sears Tower wanted it to look modern and sleek, but they also needed a material that would be lightweight and easy to maintain, so they chose aluminum. But Chicago's air pollution would discolor aluminum over time. The solution? Treat the aluminum to darken it so it wouldn't show the dirt.

"Stone, the natural material, touches the ground, and glass, the artificial material, touches the sky."
—HELMUT JAHN, ARCHITECT, MESSETURM (PAGE 35)

Scotia Plaza • Toronto, Canada • 1989

TAKE THE CHALLENGE!

Make Cladding for Your Skyscraper

Now you're ready to put on the curtain wall, or cladding — the exterior of your skyscraper. Perhaps you'd like to paint masonry (stone or brick) cladding for your building. Or, if you prefer a sleek modern metal exterior, use aluminum foil. Experiment with different looks to decide what you prefer, then use enough of that style of cladding to cover your frame.

Materials

- Newspaper
- White paper
- Old toothbrush (for granite)
- Paints, different colors
- Paper towels
- Paintbrush (for marble)
- Aluminum foil (for metal)
- Tape or glue

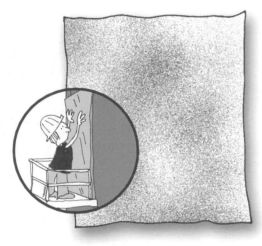

Spread newspaper to protect your work surface and lay the paper on it.

For granite: Dip the toothbrush in gray or brown paint and dab it on a paper towel. Holding the brush over the white paper, use your finger to flick paint onto the paper in a speckle pattern. Move the brush around to cover the paper. Let it dry. Then flick on *another color, red, orange, or black, for example, to make the variations in color that make stone cladding so attractive.*

For marble: Paint the paper one color and then make thick and thin streaks of a lighter color over it (white streaks on a gray background, for example).

For brick: Paint your paper dark red and let it dry. Then, draw lines as shown.

Before you attach the cladding, put in doors and windows. You can draw them on the cladding or cut them out and cover them by taping plastic wrap (on the back side of the cladding). You're the designer — all the choices and decisions are yours! Then, tape or glue the curtain wall to the frame.

A Community in the Sky

To be truly successful, a skyscraper has to do more than just stand up to its heavy load and high winds. It has to do more than look beautiful or breathtaking. In the end, skyscrapers are about more than technology and style — they are about people.

All day long, people scurry in, out, and around a skyscraper, up and down the elevators, in and out of the offices, restaurants, and shops. And there are the crowds of tourists: 1.5 million of them visit the Sears Tower every year, and the Empire State Building gets more than twice that many! Thousands more live and work in the shadow of the skyscraper, and walk by the building every day, so they, too, are affected by it, even if they never go inside!

A successful skyscraper "community" serves the needs of the people who live and work inside and around it. Its presence must be a positive contribution to urban life. A tall order for a tall building!

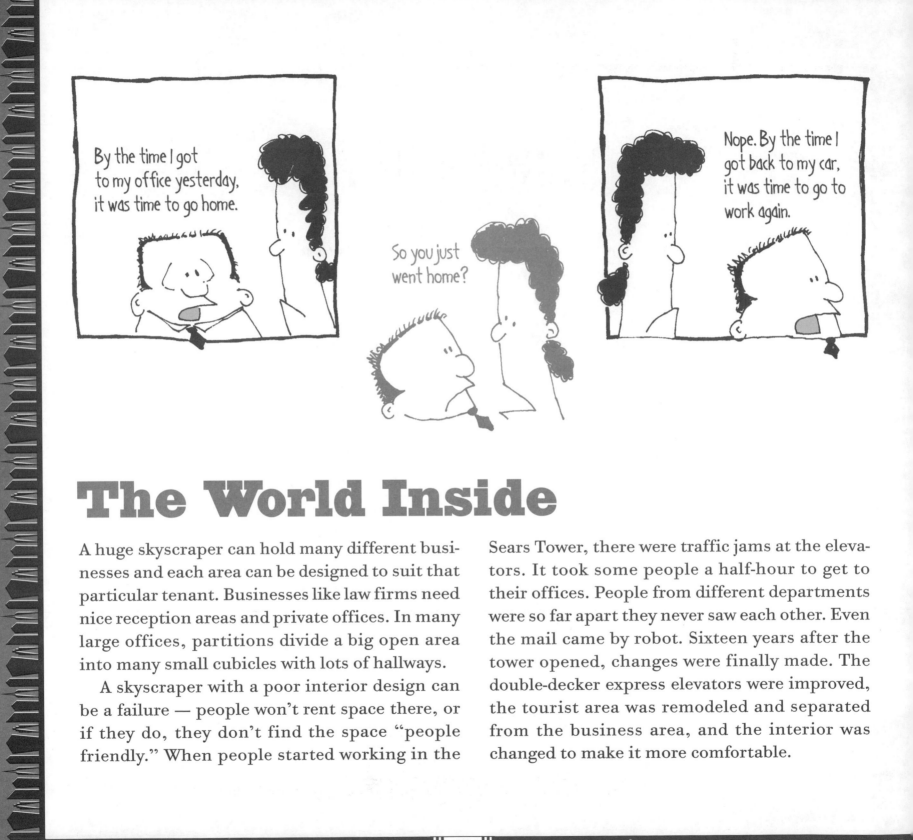

The World Inside

A huge skyscraper can hold many different businesses and each area can be designed to suit that particular tenant. Businesses like law firms need nice reception areas and private offices. In many large offices, partitions divide a big open area into many small cubicles with lots of hallways.

A skyscraper with a poor interior design can be a failure — people won't rent space there, or if they do, they don't find the space "people friendly." When people started working in the Sears Tower, there were traffic jams at the elevators. It took some people a half-hour to get to their offices. People from different departments were so far apart they never saw each other. Even the mail came by robot. Sixteen years after the tower opened, changes were finally made. The double-decker express elevators were improved, the tourist area was remodeled and separated from the business area, and the interior was changed to make it more comfortable.

Lost in a Maze

On graph paper, draw a large rectangle to represent one floor of a skyscraper. Draw a small office on one side of the rectangle for your starting point and draw the elevator in the center — that's your way out. Now, fill in the rest of the rectangle with a maze of confusing cubicles and hallways. Try to draw the maze so there's only one successful way to get to the elevator: Make some of your hallways end in an office or at a wall and have others loop around so you come back to where you started. Then challenge friends and family to find their way out. If each cubicle was an office for one person, how many people could work on this floor?

Now, see if you can fix that floor plan and create an office where you'd like to work. Start with a new rectangle and plan out a logical arrangement of offices, with shared spaces like conference rooms connected by hallways leading to the elevators. Where would you put the restrooms? How about the water coolers or a snack room? How many people can work on this floor now?

Keeping Up a Skyscraper: Who Does What

When do you think it would be easiest to do most of the daily maintenance on a skyscraper? That's right — at night! When the office workers have all gone home, (or if it's a hotel or apartment building, when most people are asleep), the workday is just beginning for a whole crew of maintenance workers.

"It's a very terrific job. We get to help clean one of the biggest skyscrapers in the world."
—CUSTODIAN,
EMPIRE STATE BUILDING

ENGINEERS inspect the elevators and heating and ventilation systems to replace any broken parts. PLUMBERS check the restrooms to fix any leaks.

SECURITY OFFICERS prowl the floors, checking that doors to private offices are locked and making sure security cameras are working properly. Meanwhile, CUSTODIANS and other workers polish floors, vacuum carpets, scrub toilets, water plants, change burned-out light bulbs, and collect the trash.

At dawn, dozens of trucks roll up to a skyscraper's loading dock. DELIVERY PEOPLE unload office supplies or food and supplies for the restaurants and cafeterias in the building.

SANITATION WORKERS pick up garbage. MAIL CARRIERS deliver hundreds of letters and packages to the building's mailroom just in time for the morning rush hour!

One Season — All Year Round!

Whether it's a snowstorm or a hot, sticky summer day, inside a modern skyscraper it's always the same — winter, spring, summer, or fall. In fact, if you don't have an office with a window, you could go all day without having any idea what the weather is like outside!

Sealed from the outside world by its curtain wall and windows that can't be opened, a skyscraper has a huge air-handling system that maintains a comfortable atmosphere inside. A network of aluminum ducts run through the spaces above the ceilings. Like your body's circulatory system, the duct system brings fresh, filtered air, at just the right temperature and humidity, to all parts of the building while removing the stale air.

Aluminum ducks? Maybe that's why they never rust...

Keeping an Eye on the Sky

Have you ever seen a movie about a space-flight that shows "mission control" — a roomful of people watching computer screens and TV monitors? Many skyscrapers have a similar kind of "command center" with walls lined with TVs and computer screens. Engineers rely on computers to monitor the equipment that keeps the building working properly. Computers check the amount and temperature of the air entering and leaving the building's huge air-conditioning units. They can tell whether a sink in one of the restrooms is leaking or if the lights in an office have been left on.

Security personnel also depend on computers. They use them to track the pictures taken by cameras set up around the building. The security officer on duty can see what's happening and, if necessary, can direct police officers or medical personnel to a problem. The Rialto Towers (page 49) in Australia, for example, has an advanced high-tech system that monitors security and safety throughout the building.

How Much Trash?

Collect the trash in your home for one day. Use a bathroom scale to weigh it. Now, imagine a skyscraper with 1,000 apartments. The family in each apartment creates the same amount of trash every day as your family does. How much trash do the garbage collectors have to cart off every day? How much trash does the building generate every year?

wow!

The Empire State Building produces about 100 tons (91 t) of garbage per month. That is equivalent to the weight of about 20 adult elephants!

That's a lot of garbage!

Do You Do Windows?

How would you like to have to wash the 16,100 windows in the Sears Tower? Luckily, no one has to. The Tower uses six robots to clean the outside of the building eight times a year. Each robot sits on the roof of a setback. An operator lines up the robot with tracks along the sides of the building. The robot lowers a washing machine on cables down the tracks. The washer squirts suds-free detergent at the windows, then scrubs, rinses, and vacuums off the water. It even cleans and recycles the dirty water.

Try it! *Have someone time you washing a window in your house. At that rate, how long would it take you to wash all of them? Now, imagine washing the 6,500 windows in the Empire State Building by hand!*

"I'll be working away, and a gust of wind will come screaming up and for a moment I'll be doing a tap dance on nothing. Then as my feet find the sill again, maybe another blast will come from above and make my knees buckle. Anyway, it keeps me interested!"
—*RICHARD HART, HEAD OF THE WINDOW-WASHING TEAM, EMPIRE STATE BUILDING, 1937*

Putting Out the Welcome Mat

One important way to make such a huge building feel "people friendly" rather than overwhelming is to have an entrance that invites people in. An attractively decorated lobby is very welcoming; many people find plants and the sound of rushing water restful and appealing.

The lobby of the Chrysler Building is lined with African red marble and the elevator doors are inlaid with cherry wood. Off the main lobby of the Sears Tower is a giant, colorful, constantly moving mobile named *"Universe,"* designed by the famous American sculptor Alexander Calder. People like to gather in the lobby near the mobile. It fascinates them to watch its silent dance. One New York City 'scraper has a waterfall cascading down a wall. At one time the *Peachtree Plaza*, a hotel in Atlanta, Georgia, actually had a lake in the lobby!

Empire State Building lobby

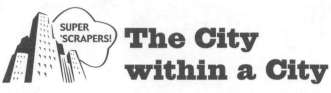

The City within a City

Rockefeller Center — home of Radio City Music Hall and the famous giant Christmas tree — is a grouping of skyscrapers and public spaces in the middle of New York City that was built in the 1930s. The centerpiece of the complex is the 70-story *General Electric* (formerly the *RCA*) *Building*. Clad in Indiana limestone, its setback design fits its surroundings beautifully and doesn't dominate the area. The other tall buildings in the complex are arranged along several city blocks in a T shape.

But what makes the complex so successful, what attracts millions of visitors every year, are the many plazas, sculptures, and shops (some 200 of them!) tucked in and around the skyscrapers. There's Radio City, the largest movie theater in the city, known throughout the world for its high-stepping dancers, the Rockettes. There's a skating rink that turns into an outdoor cafe in the summer, and there are gardens that change with the seasons, flags heralding people the world over, and benches for people-watchers of all ages. These are 'scrapers that let people know they are welcome and very important to the life of the buildings.

Rockefeller Center's skating rink was such a hit that *1000 Rue de la Gauchetière*, the tallest building in Montreal, Canada, put an elegant, modern rink inside and surrounded it with restaurants and shops.

"What monuments we leave behind in the form of buildings reveal more clearly than anything else the value we place on the quality of life."
—*HUGH STUBBINS, ARCHITECT, CITICORP CENTER*

Rockefeller Center • New York, NY • 1939

TAKE THE CHALLENGE!

Would You Live In This Neighborhood?

The tallest skyscraper in the American West, *First Interstate World Center* in Los Angeles, opened in 1990. Its site, squeezed in between other buildings, includes the city's Central Library, an historic landmark. The architects designed the skyscraper as a cylinder so it curves away from the library and other buildings and seems less overbearing. They created a public space called Bunker Hill Steps that connects two business areas that used to be separated by a wall. Not only did the architects design a building, they worked hard to improve the overall area and create an inviting urban space.

Think about Rockefeller Center and the First Interstate World Center. Think back to Citicorp Center (page 32) as another successful skyscraper complex.

Now, look back at your own skyscraper and its location in your model city. Did you make the neighborhood a better place?

Materials

- Section of sturdy cardboard in the shape of your skyscraper's site
- Scissors
- Masking tape
- Construction paper, various colors
- Cereal-box cardboard
- Glue

continued

1 Look back at your original design sketches and consider the area around your sky-scraper — is this community in the sky a friendly place that welcomes visitors? Here are some additional things to consider: Is the entrance to your building welcoming? How could you improve it? Are there places nearby for people-watchers to sit? Places for street vendors to sell their wares? How about sunny spots for office workers who want to sit outside on their lunch break? Make changes to your design, as space allows, incorporating a plaza, planters, benches, perhaps a fountain, to be sure you've created a public-friendly space.

2 Place your model on the cardboard (approximately where your skyscraper is located on the site in your design sketch) and trace around it. Cut out that section so the cardboard fits around the skyscraper foundation (you may need an adult helper). Set the skyscraper in the hole and tape it in place from below.

Now, use cardboard and construction paper to construct the neighborhood around your site.

"Whenever you finish a project you always want a second bite at it. You know yourself whether you took advantage of the opportunity to be creative or just let it slip through your fingers."
—SIR NORMAN FOSTER, ARCHITECT, HONG KONG BANK

How High Can We Go?

Skyscrapers are symbols of the cities and countries in which they stand. They do more than advertise those cities — they represent power, progress, and prosperity. They are icons of human achievement and spirit. As nations around the world gain wealth, more and more skyscrapers will be built. The race for the tallest will continue.

The Petronas Towers (page 36) probably won't hang on to the tallest title for long. The *Taipei Financial Center*, under construction in Taiwan, will top it in a few years. But if the Taiwanese 'scraper doesn't include a proposed spire, it could be beaten by the *Shanghai World Financial Center* in China. Not to be outdone, the Japanese are thinking about a 180-story skyscraper called *Millennium Tower*, shaped like a very long upside-down ice cream cone! Meanwhile, back in New York City, Chicago, and other American cities, there are people plotting skyscrapers to take back the title for the United States.

TALL THINKERS

Frank Lloyd Wright and His "Mile-High" 'Scraper

"Architecture ... is life itself taking form. Architecture is that great living creative spirit which from generation to generation, from age to age ... creates, according to the nature of man and his circumstances as they change."
—FRANK LLOYD WRIGHT, ARCHITECT

In 1956, one of the most famous American architects, **Frank Lloyd Wright**, drew up plans for a skyscraper that actually reached a mile (1.6 km) into the sky! With an incredible 528 stories, it would have room for up to 200,000 people. As Wright imagined it, it wouldn't be a village in the sky, it would be an entire city! Inside would be offices, apartments, schools, medical clinics, sports facilities, and shops. Its 56 elevators would be powered by atomic energy. You name it, and this skyscraper would have it! To think about it — let alone see it — would be breathtaking! His drawings are a testimony to his vision and talent.

Is Wright's dream of such a tall skyscraper possible with existing technology? Most experts say "Yes," we do have the know-how, skills, and materials to make it happen. In fact, there are currently designs in Japan for "sky cities," pyramid-like skyscrapers that would be almost 1 mile (1.6 km) high. Up to 1 million people could work and live in them. Inside would be homes, offices — even entire parks and trees!

Frank Lloyd Wright's *"The Mile-High Illinois"* • 1956

Reach for the Sky!

Experts wonder if building so high would be such a good idea. There are safety issues, as well as the amount and cost of the materials. And we'd have to deal with the sheer size of the building: Would people feel too isolated and alone? Would the incredible size exaggerate all the problems regular skyscrapers have? Or, would the size force technology and innovation forward?

Despite the drawbacks and all the unanswered questions, the fact that we can build tall means that we likely will. The challenges of conquering the problems and inventing new technologies are probably too hard for us to resist. And so our imaginations will continue to dream big. Lucky for us, our imaginations will help us figure out the solutions as well.

The Elevator Problem

Does it surprise you to learn that it's not the strength of the steel frame that limits the height of skyscrapers, it's the speed and arrangement of elevators? Every time skyscrapers get significantly taller, express elevators need to travel even faster to get people to higher floors in a short time. But when people travel vertically too fast, their eardrums pop, their stomachs lurch, and their knees buckle from the very quick acceleration and gravity's pull. On the other hand, if you put in too many skylobbies and make people change elevators too often, people won't want to rent the upper floors. Any way you look at it, it's another problem for the engineers — or you — to figure out!

The World of Skyscrapers

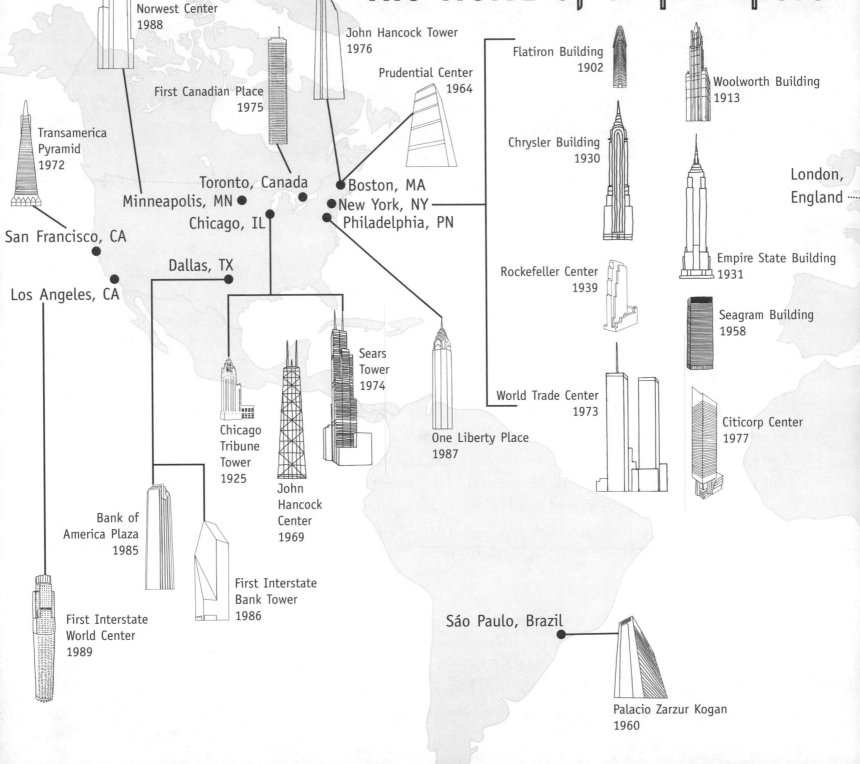

Norwest Center
1988

John Hancock Tower
1976

Prudential Center
1964

Flatiron Building
1902

Woolworth Building
1913

First Canadian Place
1975

Transamerica
Pyramid
1972

Chrysler Building
1930

Toronto, Canada

Boston, MA

Minneapolis, MN

New York, NY

Chicago, IL

Philadelphia, PN

San Francisco, CA

London,
England

Dallas, TX

Rockefeller Center
1939

Empire State Building
1931

Los Angeles, CA

Sears
Tower
1974

Seagram Building
1958

Chicago
Tribune
Tower
1925

World Trade Center
1973

Citicorp Center
1977

Bank of
America Plaza
1985

John
Hancock
Center
1969

One Liberty Place
1987

First Interstate
Bank Tower
1986

First Interstate
World Center
1989

Sáo Paulo, Brazil

Palacio Zarzur Kogan
1960

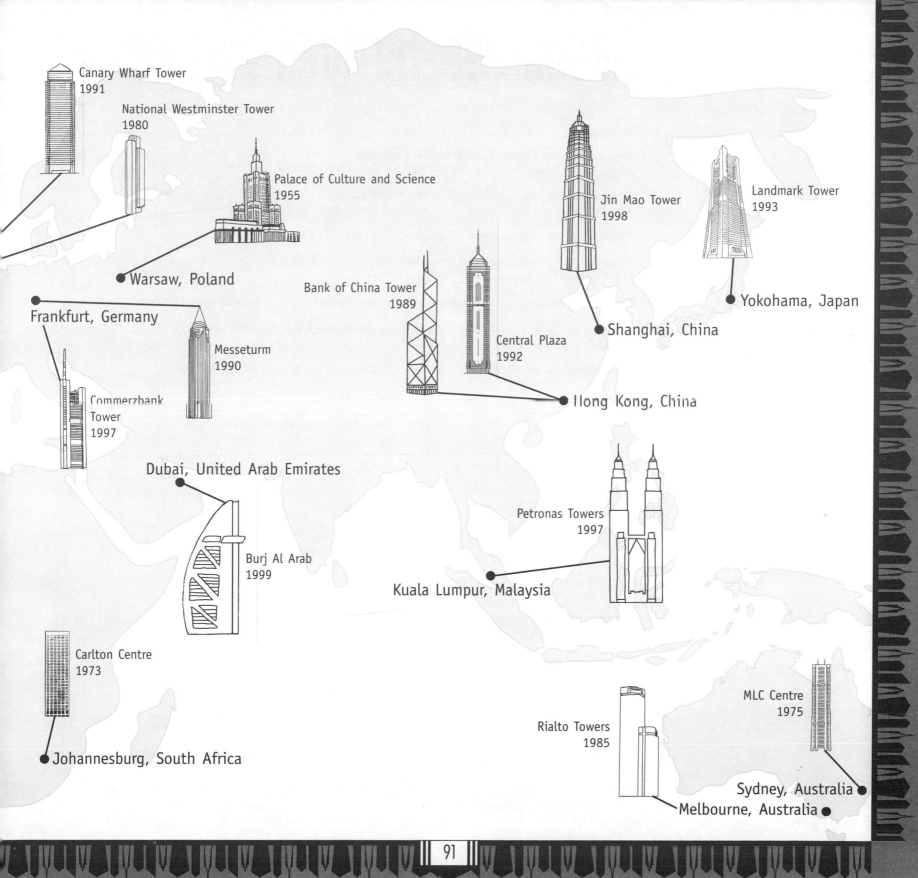

Canary Wharf Tower
1991

National Westminster Tower
1980

Palace of Culture and Science
1955

Jin Mao Tower
1998

Landmark Tower
1993

Warsaw, Poland

Bank of China Tower
1989

Yokohama, Japan

Frankfurt, Germany

Messeturm
1990

Central Plaza
1992

Shanghai, China

Commerzbank
Tower
1997

Ilong Kong, China

Dubai, United Arab Emirates

Petronas Towers
1997

Burj Al Arab
1999

Kuala Lumpur, Malaysia

Carlton Centre
1973

MLC Centre
1975

Rialto Towers
1985

Johannesburg, South Africa

Sydney, Australia

Melbourne, Australia

Resources for Kids

Books

Doherty, Craig A., and Katherine M. Doherty.
The Empire State Building, Building America. Blackbirch Press, 1998.

Doherty, Craig A., and Katherine M. Doherty.
The Sears Tower, Building America. Blackbirch, Press, 1995.

Dupré, Judith. *Skyscrapers*. Black Dog & Leventhal Publishers, 1996.

Jennings, Terry. *Cranes, Dump Trucks, Bulldozers and Other Building Machines*,
How Things Work. Kingfisher Books, 1993.

Michael, Duncan. *How Skyscrapers Are Made.* Facts On File Publications, 1987.

Oxlade, Chris. *Skyscrapers & Towers*, Superstructures. Raintree Steck-Vaughn
Publishers, 1997.

Salvadori, Mario. *The Art of Construction.* Chicago Review Press, 1990.

Sauvain, Philip. *Skyscrapers*, How We Build. Garrett Educational Corporation, 1990.

Severance, John B. *Skyscrapers: How America Grew Up.* Holiday House, 2000.

Websites

Building Big
www.buildingbig.com

The Empire State Building (official site)
www.esbnyc.com

The History Channel: Skyscrapers
www.historychannel.com/exhibits/skyscrapers

The Sears Tower (official site)
www.sears-tower.com

The Skyscraper Museum
www.skyscraper.org

Top of the World Trade Center
www.wtc-top.com
*For a scrollable 360° panarama of the view
from the Top of the World, click on* The
Experience, *then on* New York skyline.

World's Tallest Buildings
www.worldstallest.com

**Descriptions/photographs of famous
skyscrapers around the world**
www.GreatBuildings.com

Videos

Building Big: Skyscrapers, produced by WGBH Boston Video, 60 minutes, WGBH,
2000, videocassette

Skyscrapers: Going Up, produced by Unapix Consumer Products, 52 minutes, Discovery
Channel, 2000, videocassette

Index

More Good Books from Williamson Publishing